ECONOMIC AND SOCIAL COMMISSION
FOR WESTERN ASIA (ESCWA)

اللجنة الاقتصادية والاجتماعية
لغربي آسيا (الإسكوا)

نشرة السكان والإحصاءات الحيوية في منطقة الإسكوا

BULLETIN ON POPULATION AND VITAL STATISTICS IN THE ESCWA REGION

العدد الثاني عشر
Twelfth Issue

الأمم المتحدة
نيويورك، ٢٠٠٩

UNITED NATIONS
New York, 2009

UNITED NATIONS PUBLICATION
E/ESCWA/SD/2009/15
ISBN. 978-92-1-128334-1
ISSN. 1020-7368
Sales No. B.10.II.L.4
09-0562

Contents

المحتويات

	الصفحة / Page
Introduction .... مقدمة	1
Part I: Population .... الفصل الأول: السكان	3
Part II: Fertility and Mortality .... الفصل الثاني: الخصوبة والوفيات	57
Part III: Marriage and Divorce .... الفصل الثالث: الزواج والطلاق	97
Technical Notes .... الملاحظات الفنية	107
Glossary of Statistical Terms .... مسرد المصطلحات الإحصائية	113

Annex 1: International Classification of Causes of Death .... ملحق 1: التصنيف الدولي لأسباب الوفاة	95

List of tables

قائمة الجداول

Part I: Population

الفصل الأول: السكان

Table 1.	Population estimates in ESCWA Region compared to other regions in 1990, 1995, 2000, 2005 and 2009 (in 000s) .... جدول 1- تقديرات السكان في منطقة الإسكوا مقارنة لمناطق أخرى خلال (بالآلاف) 2009 و 2005 و 2000 و 1995 و 1990	5
Table 2.	Population estimates (in 000s), (1990-2009) .... جدول 2- تقديرات السكان (بالآلاف) ، (1990-2009)	6
Table 3.	International migrant stock in ESCWA countries and other regions, 1990, 1995, 2000, 2005 and 2010 .... جدول 3- مخزون المهاجرين في بلدان الإسكوا مقارنة بمناطق أخرى، 2010 و 2005 و 2000 و 1995 و 1990	7
Table 4.	Life expectancy at birth, 1990-1995, 1995-2000, 2000-2005 and 2005-2010 .... جدول 4- العمر المتوقع عند الولادة 1990-1995 و 2000-1995 و 2005-2000 و 2010-2005	8
Table 5.	Sex ratio at birth, 1990-1995, 1995-2000, 2000-2005 and 2005-2010 .... جدول 5- نسبة الجنسين عند الولادة، 1990-1995 و 2000-1995 و 2005-2000 و 2010-2005	9

		الصفحة Page
Table 6.	Population of Bahrain by age group, 1991 census	10
Table 7.	Population of Bahrain by age group, 2001 census	11
Table 8.	Population of Egypt by age group, 1986 census	12
Table 9.	Population of Egypt by age group, 1996 census	13
Table 10.	Population of Egypt by age group, 2006 census	14
Table 11.	Population of Iraq by age group, 1987 census	15
Table 12.	Population of Iraq by age group, 1997 census	16
Table 13.	Population of Jordan by age group, 1994 census	17
Table 14.	Population of Jordan by age group, 2004 census	18
Table 15.	Population of Kuwait by age group, 1985 census	19
Table 16.	Population of Kuwait by age group, 1995 census	20
Table 17.	Population of Kuwait by age group, 2005 census	21
Table 18.	Population of Oman by age group, 1993 census	22
Table 19.	Population of Oman by age group, 2003 census	23
Table 20.	Population of Palestine by age group, 1997 census	24
Table 21.	Population of Palestine by age group, 2007 census	25
Table 22.	Population of Qatar by age group, 1986 census	26
Table 23.	Population of Qatar by age group, 2004 census	27
Table 24.	Population of Saudi Arabia by age group, 1992 census	28

	الصفحة
جدول 6-	السكان في البحرين بحسب الفئة العمرية، تعداد 1991 ....
جدول 7-	السكان في البحرين بحسب الفئة العمرية، تعداد 2001 ....
جدول 8-	السكان في مصر بحسب الفئة العمرية، تعداد 1986 ....
جدول 9-	السكان في مصر بحسب الفئة العمرية، تعداد 1996 ....
جدول 10-	السكان في مصر بحسب الفئة العمرية، تعداد 2006 ....
جدول 11-	السكان في العراق بحسب الفئة العمرية، تعداد 1987 ....
جدول 12-	السكان في العراق بحسب الفئة العمرية، تعداد 1997 ....
جدول 13-	السكان في الأردن بحسب الفئة العمرية، تعداد 1994 ....
جدول 14-	السكان في الأردن بحسب الفئة العمرية، تعداد 2004 ....
جدول 15-	السكان في الكويت بحسب الفئة العمرية، تعداد 1985 ....
جدول 16-	السكان في الكويت بحسب الفئة العمرية، تعداد 1995 ....
جدول 17-	السكان في الكويت بحسب الفئة العمرية، تعداد 2005 ....
جدول 18-	السكان في عمان بحسب الفئة العمرية، تعداد 1993 ....
جدول 19-	السكان في عمان بحسب الفئة العمرية، تعداد 2003 ....
جدول 20-	السكان في فلسطين بحسب الفئة العمرية، تعداد 1997 ....
جدول 21-	السكان في فلسطين بحسب الفئة العمرية، تعداد 2007 ....
جدول 22-	السكان في قطر بحسب الفئة العمرية، تعداد 1986 ....
جدول 23-	السكان في قطر بحسب الفئة العمرية، تعداد 2004 ....
جدول 24-	السكان في المملكة العربية السعودية بحسب الفئة العمرية، تعداد 2004 ....

	الصفحة Page
جدول 25- السكان في المملكة العربية السعودية بحسب الفئة العمرية، تعداد 2004	29
جدول 26- السكان في السودان بحسب الفئة العمرية، تعداد 1993	30
جدول 27- السكان في السودان بحسب الفئة العمرية، تعداد 2008	31
جدول 28- السكان في الجمهورية العربية السورية بحسب الفئة العمرية، تعداد 1994	32
جدول 29- السكان في الجمهورية العربية السورية بحسب الفئة العمرية، تعداد 2004	33
جدول 30- السكان في الإمارات العربية المتحدة بحسب الفئة العمرية، تعداد 1985	34
جدول 31- السكان في الإمارات العربية المتحدة بحسب الفئة العمرية، تعداد 1995	35
جدول 32- السكان في الإمارات العربية المتحدة بحسب الفئة العمرية، تعداد 2005	36
جدول 33- السكان في اليمن بحسب الفئة العمرية، تعداد 1994	37
جدول 34- السكان في اليمن بحسب الفئة العمرية، تعداد 2004	38
جدول 35- التعدادات السكانية (مواطنون، غير مواطنين) (حضر، ريف): البحرين	39
جدول 36- التعدادات السكانية (مواطنون، غير مواطنين) (حضر، ريف): مصر	39
جدول 37- التعدادات السكانية (مواطنون، غير مواطنين) (حضر، ريف): العراق	39

Table 25. Population of Saudi Arabia by age group, 2004 census 29

Table 26. Population of Sudan by age group, 1993 census 30

Table 27. Population of Sudan by age group, 2008 census 31

Table 28. Population of Syrian Arab Republic by age group, 1994 census 32

Table 29. Population of Syrian Arab Republic by age group, 2004 census 33

Table 30. Population of United Arab Emirates by age group, 1985 census 34

Table 31. Population of United Arab Emirates by age group, 1995 census 35

Table 32. Population of United Arab Emirates by age group, 2005 census 36

Table 33. Population of Yemen by age group, 1994 census 37

Table 34. Population of Yemen by age group, 2004 census 38

Table 35. Population censuses (nationals, non-nationals) (urban, rural): Bahrain 39

Table 36. Population censuses (nationals, non-nationals) (urban, rural): Egypt 39

Table 37. Population censuses (nationals, non-nationals) (urban, rural): Iraq 39

		الصفحة Page
جدول 38- التعدادات السكانية (مواطنون، غير مواطنين) (حضر، ريف): الأردن	Table 38. Population censuses (nationals, non-nationals) (urban, rural): Jordan	40
جدول 39- التعدادات السكانية (مواطنون، غير مواطنين) (حضر، ريف): الكويت	Table 39. Population censuses (nationals, non-nationals) (urban, rural): Kuwait	40
جدول 40- التعدادات السكانية (مواطنون، غير مواطنين) (حضر، ريف): عمان	Table 40. Population censuses (nationals, non-nationals) (urban, rural): Oman	40
جدول 41- التعدادات السكانية (مواطنون، غير مواطنين) (حضر، ريف): فلسطين	Table 41. Population censuses (nationals, non-nationals) (urban, rural): Palestine	41
جدول 42- التعدادات السكانية (مواطنون، غير مواطنين) (حضر، ريف): قطر	Table 42. Population censuses (nationals, non-nationals) (urban, rural): Qatar	41
جدول 43- التعدادات السكانية (مواطنون، غير مواطنين) (حضر، ريف): المملكة العربية السعودية	Table 43. Population censuses (nationals, non-nationals) (urban, rural): Saudi Arabia	41
جدول 44- التعدادات السكانية (مواطنون، غير مواطنين) (حضر، ريف): السودان	Table 44. Population censuses (nationals, non-nationals) (urban, rural): Sudan	42
جدول 45- التعدادات السكانية (مواطنون، غير مواطنين) (حضر، ريف): الجمهورية العربية السورية	Table 45. Population censuses (nationals, non-nationals) (urban, rural): Syrian Arab Republic	42
جدول 46- التعدادات السكانية (مواطنون، غير مواطنين) (حضر، ريف): الإمارات العربية المتحدة	Table 46. Population censuses (nationals, non-nationals) (urban, rural): United Arab Emirates	42
جدول 47- التعدادات السكانية (مواطنون، غير مواطنين) (حضر، ريف): اليمن	Table 47. Population censuses (nationals, non-nationals) (urban, rural): Yemen	43
جدول 48- النسبة المئوية للشباب (في الفئة العمرية 15-24) لمجموع السكان خلال سنوات التعداد	Table 48. Percentage of youth population (in the age group 15-24) to total population during the census years	44
جدول 49- النسبة المئوية للشباب (في الفئة العمرية 15-24) للسكان العاملين (في الفئة العمرية 64-15) خلال سنوات التعداد	Table 49. Percentage of youth population (in the age group 15-24) to working population (in the age group) during the census years	45

	الصفحة Page

جدول 50- النسبة المئوية للمسنين (في الفئة العمرية 65+) لمجموع السكان خلال سنوات التعداد 46

جدول 51- النسبة المئوية للإعالة لمجموع السكان خلال سنوات التعداد 47

الفصل الثاني: الخصوبة والوفيات

جدول 52- المواليد الأحياء في بلدان الإسكوا 1990-2008 59

جدول 53- معدل المواليد الأحياء الخام لكل ألف نسمة من السكان في بلدان الإسكوا 1990-2008 59

جدول 54- الوفيات في بلدان الإسكوا 1990-2008 60

جدول 55- معدل الوفيات الخام لكل ألف نسمة من الولادات في بلدان الإسكوا 1990-2008 60

جدول 56- معدل الزيادة الطبيعية لكل مائة من السكان في بلدان الإسكوا 1990-2008 61

جدول 57- وفيات الأجنة في بلدان الإسكوا 1990-2008 65

جدول 58- معدل وفيات الأجنة لكل ألف من الولادات الحية في بلدان الإسكوا 1990-2008 65

جدول 59- وفيات الرضع في بلدان الإسكوا 1990-2008 66

جدول 60- معدل وفيات الرضع لكل ألف من الولادات الحية في بلدان الإسكوا 1990-2008 66

جدول 61- وفيات الأطفال في بلدان الإسكوا 1990-2008 67

جدول 62- معدل وفيات الأطفال لكل ألف من الولادات الحية في بلدان الإسكوا 1990-2008 67

Table 50. Percentage of elderly population (in the age group 65+) to total population during the census years 46

Table 51. Percentage of dependency to total population during the census years 47

Part II: Fertility and Mortality

Table 52. Live Births in ESCWA Countries 1990-2008 59

Table 53. Crude Birth Rate (per '000) population in ESCWA Countries 1990-2008 59

Table 54. Deaths in ESCWA Countries 1990-2008 60

Table 55. Crude Death Rate (per'000) Live Births in ESCWA Countries 1990-2008 60

Table 56. Rate of Natural Increase (per '00) population in ESCWA Countries 1990-2008 61

Table 57. Foetal deaths in ESCWA countries 1990-2008 65

Table 58. Foetal Mortality Rate (per '000) Live Births in ESCWA countries 1990-2008 65

Table 59. Infant deaths in ESCWA countries 1990-2008 66

Table 60. Infant Mortality Rate (per'000) Live Births in ESCWA countries 1990-2008 66

Table 61. Child deaths in ESCWA countries 1990-2008 67

Table 62. Child Mortality Rate (per'000) Live Births in ESCWA countries 1990-2008 67

	الصفحة Page

Table 63. General Fertility, Total Fertility, Adolescent Fertility, Gross Reproduction Rates, and Mean Age of Childbearing since 1990 .... **73**

Table 64. Registered Deaths by Cause: Crude Rates and Per Cent........... **77**

Part III: Marriage and Divorce

Table 65. Marriages in ESCWA countries 1990-2008................ **99**

Table 66. Crude Marriage Rate (per'000) population in ESCWA countries 1990-2008........ **99**

Table 67. Divorces in ESCWA countries 1990-2008................ **100**

Table 68. Crude Divorce Rate (per'000) population in ESCWA countries 1990-2008........ **100**

Table 69. Mean age at First Marriage in ESCWA countries............... **103**

List of Figures

Fig 1. Population estimates of ESCWA Region compared to other regions in 2009 .... **5**

Fig 2. Bahrain population pyramid, 2001 census **48**

Fig 3. Bahrain population pyramid, 1991 census **48**

Fig 4. Egypt population pyramid, 2006 census **49**

Fig 5. Egypt population pyramid, 1996 census **49**

جدول 63- معدل الخصوبة العام، ومعدل الخصوبة الكلي لدى المراهقات ومعدل الإحلال الإجمالي، ومتوسط عمر المرأة عند الإنجاب منذ عام 1990 ....

جدول 64- أسباب الوفيات المسجلة: المعدل الخام و النسبة في المئة ....

الفصل الثالث: الزواج والطلاق

جدول 65- الزواج في بلدان الإسكوا 2008-1990 ....

جدول 66- معدل الزواج الخام لكل ألف من السكان في بلدان الإسكوا 2008-1990..............

جدول 67- الطلاق في بلدان الإسكوا 2008-1990..............

جدول 68- معدل الطلاق الخام لكل ألف من السكان في بلدان الإسكوا 2008-1990..............

جدول 69- متوسط العمر عند الزواج الأول في بلدان الإسكوا..............

قائمة الأشكال

شكل 1- تقديرات السكان في منطقة الإسكوا مقارنة بمناطق أخرى في عام 2009..............

شكل 2- الهرم السكاني للبحرين، تعداد 2001 ....

شكل 3- الهرم السكاني للبحرين، تعداد 1991 ....

شكل 4- الهرم السكاني لمصر، تعداد 2006 ....

شكل 5- الهرم السكاني لمصر، تعداد 1996 ....

		العربية	English	

شكل -6	الهرم السكاني لمصر ، تعداد 1986	49	Fig 6.	Egypt population pyramid, 1986 census ....
شكل -7	الهرم السكاني للعراق ، تعداد 1997	50	Fig 7.	Iraq population pyramid, 1997 census ....
شكل -8	الهرم السكاني للعراق ، تعداد 1987	50	Fig 8.	Iraq population pyramid, 1987 census ....
شكل -9	الهرم السكاني للأردن ، تعداد 2004	50	Fig 9.	Jordan population pyramid, 2004 census ....
شكل -10	الهرم السكاني للأردن ، تعداد 1994	50	Fig 10.	Jordan population pyramid, 1994 census ....
شكل -11	الهرم السكاني للكويت ، تعداد 2005	51	Fig 11.	Kuwait population pyramid, 2005 census ....
شكل -12	الهرم السكاني للكويت ، تعداد 1995	51	Fig 12.	Kuwait population pyramid, 1995 census ....
شكل -13	الهرم السكاني للكويت ، تعداد 1985	51	Fig 13.	Kuwait population pyramid, 1985 census ....
شكل -14	الهرم السكاني لعمان ، تعداد 2003	52	Fig 14.	Oman population pyramid, 2003 census ....
شكل -15	الهرم السكاني لعمان ، تعداد 1993	52	Fig 15.	Oman population pyramid, 1993 census ....
شكل -16	الهرم السكاني لفلسطين ، تعداد 2007	52	Fig 16.	Palestine population pyramid, 2007 census ....
شكل -17	الهرم السكاني لفلسطين ، تعداد 1997	52	Fig 17.	Palestine population pyramid, 1997 census ....
شكل -18	الهرم السكاني لقطر ، تعداد 2004	53	Fig 18.	Qatar population pyramid, 2004 census ....
شكل -19	الهرم السكاني لقطر ، تعداد 1986	53	Fig 19.	Qatar population pyramid, 1986 census ....
شكل -20	الهرم السكاني للمملكة العربية السعودية، تعداد 2004	53	Fig 20.	Saudi Arabia population pyramid, 2004 census ....
شكل -21	الهرم السكاني للمملكة العربية السعودية، تعداد 1992	53	Fig 21.	Saudi Arabia population pyramid, 1992 census ....
شكل -22	الهرم السكاني للسودان، تعداد 1993	54	Fig 22.	Sudan population pyramid, 2008 census ....
شكل -23	الهرم السكاني للسودان، تعداد 2008	54	Fig 23.	Sudan population pyramid, 1993 census ....
شكل -24	الهرم السكاني للجمهورية العربية السورية، تعداد 2004	54	Fig 24.	Syrian Arab Republic population pyramid, 2004 census ....
شكل -25	الهرم السكاني للجمهورية العربية السورية، تعداد 1994	54	Fig 25.	Syrian Arab Republic population pyramid, 1994 census ....
شكل -26	الهرم السكاني للإمارات العربية المتحدة، تعداد 2005	55	Fig 26.	United Arab Emirates population pyramid, 2005 census ....

Fig 27.	United Arab Emirates population pyramid, 1995 census.....	55	.... تعداد 1995 الهرم السكاني للإمارات العربية المتحدة، تعداد	شكل -27
Fig 28.	United Arab Emirates population pyramid, 1985 census.....	55	.... تعداد 1985 الهرم السكاني للإمارات العربية المتحدة، تعداد	شكل -28
Fig 29.	Yemen population pyramid, 2004 census	56	.... تعداد 2004 الهرم السكاني لليمن، تعداد	شكل -29
Fig 30.	Yemen pyramid, 1994 census	56	.... تعداد 1994 الهرم السكاني لليمن، تعداد	شكل -30
Fig 31.	Rate of natural increase in Bahrain ,1990-2008	62	.... 1990-2008 معدل الزيادة الطبيعية في البحرين،	شكل -31
Fig 32.	Rate of natural increase in Egypt, 1990-2008	62	.... 1990-2008 معدل الزيادة الطبيعية في مصر،	شكل -32
Fig 33.	Rate of natural increase in Iraq, 1990-2008	62	.... 1990-2008 معدل الزيادة الطبيعية في العراق،	شكل -33
Fig 34.	Rate of natural increase in Jordan, 1990-2008	62	.... 1990-2008 معدل الزيادة الطبيعية في الأردن،	شكل -34
Fig 35.	Rate of natural increase in Kuwait, 1990-2008	63	.... 1990-2008 معدل الزيادة الطبيعية في الكويت،	شكل -35
Fig 36.	Rate of natural increase in Lebanon, 1990-2008	63	.... 1990-2008 معدل الزيادة الطبيعية في لبنان،	شكل -36
Fig 37.	Rate of natural increase in Oman, 1990-2008	63	.... 1990-2008 معدل الزيادة الطبيعية في عمان،	شكل -37
Fig 38.	Rate of natural increase in Palestine, 1990-2008	63	.... 1990-2008 معدل الزيادة الطبيعية في فلسطين،	شكل -38
Fig 39.	Rate of natural increase in Qatar, 1990-2008	64	.... 1990-2008 معدل الزيادة الطبيعية في قطر،	شكل -39
Fig 40.	Rate of natural increase in Saudi Arabia, 1990-2008.....	64	.... 1990- 2008 معدل الزيادة الطبيعية في المملكة العربية السعودية،	شكل -40
Fig 41.	Rate of natural increase in Syrian Arab Republic, 1990-2008.....	64	.... 1990- 2008 معدل الزيادة الطبيعية في الجمهورية العربية السورية،	شكل -41
Fig 42.	Rate of natural increase in United Arab Emirates, 1990-2008.....	64	.... 1990- 2008 معدل الزيادة الطبيعية في الإمارات العربية المتحدة،	شكل -42
Fig 43.	Rate of natural increase in Yemen, 1990-2008	64	.... 1990-2008 معدل الزيادة الطبيعية في اليمن،	شكل -43
Fig 44.	Deaths, infant deaths, child deaths in ESCWA countries according to data availability in Bahrain	68	.... الوفيات، وفيات الرضع ووفيات الأطفال في بلدان الإسكوا حسب توفر البيانات في البحرين	شكل -44
Fig 45.	Deaths, infant deaths, child deaths in ESCWA countries	68	.... الوفيات، وفيات الرضع ووفيات الأطفال في بلدان الإسكوا حسب	شكل -45

شكل 46- نوفر البيانات في مصر 69
شكل 47- الوفيات، وفيات الرضع ووفيات الأطفال في بلدان الإسكوا حسب توفر البيانات في العراق 69
شكل 48- الوفيات، وفيات الرضع ووفيات الأطفال في بلدان الإسكوا حسب توفر البيانات في الكويت 70
شكل 49- الوفيات، وفيات الرضع ووفيات الأطفال في بلدان الإسكوا حسب توفر البيانات في عمان 70
شكل 50- الوفيات، وفيات الرضع ووفيات الأطفال في بلدان الإسكوا حسب توفر البيانات في فلسطين 71
شكل 51- الوفيات، وفيات الرضع ووفيات الأطفال في بلدان الإسكوا حسب توفر البيانات في قطر 71
شكل 52- الوفيات، وفيات الرضع ووفيات الأطفال في بلدان الإسكوا حسب توفر البيانات في المملكة العربية السعودية 72
شكل 53- الوفيات، وفيات الرضع ووفيات الأطفال في بلدان الإسكوا حسب توفر البيانات في الإمارات العربية المتحدة 76
شكل 54- معدل الخصوبة الكلي لكل امرأة حسب توفر البيانات 1990-2008 101
شكل 55- معدل الزواج الخام ومعدل الطلاق الخام لكل ألف من السكان في البحرين 2008-1990 101
شكل 56- معدل الزواج الخام ومعدل الطلاق الخام لكل ألف من السكان في مصر 2008-1990 101
شكل 57- معدل الزواج الخام ومعدل الطلاق الخام لكل ألف من السكان للأردن 2008-1990 101
معدل الزواج الخام ومعدل الطلاق الخام لكل ألف من السكان في لبنان 2008-1990 ....

Fig 46. according to data availability in Egypt ....

Fig 46. Deaths, infant deaths, child deaths in ESCWA countries according to data availability in Iraq ....

Fig 47. Deaths, infant deaths, child deaths in ESCWA countries according to data availability in Kuwait ....

Fig 48. Deaths, infant deaths, child deaths in ESCWA countries according to data availability in Oman ....

Fig 49. Deaths, infant deaths, child deaths in ESCWA countries according to data availability in Palestine ....

Fig 50. Deaths, infant deaths, child deaths in ESCWA countries according to data availability in Qatar ....

Fig 51. Deaths, infant deaths, child deaths in ESCWA countries according to data availability in Saudi Arabia ....

Fig 52. Deaths, infant deaths, child deaths in ESCWA countries according to data availability in United Arab Emirates ....

Fig 53. Total Fertility Rate per woman according to data availability 1990-2008 ....

Fig 54. Marriage and Divorce Crude Rates (per '000) population for member countries according to data availability 1990-2008 in Bahrain ....

Fig 55. Marriage and Divorce Crude Rates (per '000) population for member countries according to data availability 1990-2008 in Egypt ....

Fig 56. Marriage and Divorce Crude Rates (per '000) population for member countries according to data availability 1990-2008 in Jordan ....

Fig 57. Marriage and Divorce Crude Rates (per '000) population for member countries according to data availability 1990-2008 in Lebanon ....

شكل 58-	معدل الزواج الخام ومعدل الطلاق الخام لكل ألف نسمة من السكان في قطر 1990-2008	102	Fig 58. Marriage and Divorce Crude Rates (per '000) population for member countries according to data availability1990-2008 in Qatar
شكل 59-	معدل الزواج الخام ومعدل الطلاق الخام لكل ألف نسمة من السكان في المملكة العربية السعودية 1990-2008	102	Fig 59. Marriage and Divorce Crude Rates (per '000) population for member countries according to data availability1990-2008 in Saudi Arabia
شكل 60-	معدل الزواج الخام ومعدل الطلاق الخام لكل ألف نسمة من السكان في الإمارات العربية المتحدة 1990-2008	102	Fig 60. Marriage and Divorce Crude Rates (per '000) population for member countries according to data availability1990-2008 in United Arab Emirates
شكل 61-	متوسط العمر عند الزواج الأول في الأردن حسب توفر البيانات 2008-1990	104	Fig 61. Mean age at first marriage in Jordan according to data availability 1990-2008
شكل 62-	متوسط العمر عند الزواج الأول في مصر حسب توفر البيانات 2008-1990	104	Fig 62. Mean age at first marriage in Egypt according to data availability 1990-2008
شكل 63-	متوسط العمر عند الزواج الأول في قطر حسب توفر البيانات 2008-1990	104	Fig 63. Mean age at first marriage in Qatar according to data availability 1990-2008
شكل 64-	متوسط العمر عند الزواج الأول في البحرين حسب توفر البيانات 2008-1990	104	Fig 64. Mean age at first marriage in Bahrain according to data availability 1990-2008
شكل 65-	متوسط العمر عند الزواج الأول في بلدان الإسكوا حسب توفر البيانات 2008-1990 للنساء	105	Fig 65. Mean Age at First Marriage in ESCWA countries according to data availability 1990-2008, for Women
شكل 66-	متوسط العمر عند الزواج الأول في بلدان الإسكوا حسب توفر البيانات 2008-1990 للرجال	105	Fig 66. Mean Age at First Marriage in ESCWA countries according to data availability 1990-2008, for Men

رموز
Symbols

بيانات غير متوفرة	....	Data not available
ضئيل أو صفر	-	Negligible or zero

INTRODUCTION

The Economic and Social Commission for Western Asia (ESCWA) presents the twelfth issue of the Bulletin on Population and Vital Statistics in the ESCWA Region. The Bulletin provides detailed information on the population of the ESCWA region and its vital events: births, deaths, marriages and divorces. It presents this information in three parts: population; fertility and mortality; and marriage and divorce.

In this issue, the Bulletin presents the main indicators for each vital event. These indicators have been computed using national data, weighted by population estimates from the 2008 Revision of the World Population Prospects, prepared by the United Nations Department of Economic and Social Affairs. Data series for 1990, 1995 and from 2000 to the latest available year which are presented have been compiled by ESCWA from national statistical yearbooks and vital statistics publications, where available, and from responses by member countries to ESCWA questionnaires. These questionnaires are used to compile additional information from national statistical offices that reflect regional specificities.

In this current issue, major changes have been introduced to produce a completely revised Bulletin, in which both quality and relevance of disseminated data are enhanced. The objective of these changes is to provide a more effective tool for monitoring comparable data and indicators.

The electronic version of the Bulletin can be accessed on the ESCWA Statistics Division webpage at http://www.escwa.un.org/divisions/main.asp?division=sd.

ESCWA is grateful to member countries for their collaboration in producing the Bulletin.

مقدمة

تقدم اللجنة الاقتصادية والاجتماعية لغربي آسيا (الإسكوا) العدد الثاني عشر من نشرة السكان والإحصاءات الحيوية في منطقة الإسكوا، وهو يتضمن معلومات مفصلة عن السكان في المنطقة ووقائعهم الحيوية أي الولادات والوفيات والزواج والطلاق. وتعرض هذه المعلومات في ثلاثة فصول: السكان؛ والخصوبة والوفيات؛ والزواج والطلاق.

وتحتوي هذا العدد من النشرة على المؤشرات الرئيسية لكل حدث حيوي والتي تم احتسابها باستخدام البيانات الوطنية وترجيحها بتقدير ات السكان الواردة في "التوقعات السكانية في العالم: تنقيح عام 2008" التي أعدتها إدارة الشؤون الاقتصادية والاجتماعية في الأمم المتحدة. وترد في هذا العدد بيانات لسنتي 1990 و1995 وللسنوات بدءا من عام 2000 وحتى آخر سنة متوفرة. والمؤشرات التي قد جمعت من قبل الإسكوا من النشرات الإحصائية الوطنية والمنشورات حول الإحصاءات الحيوية حيثما توفرت، ومن ردود البلدان الأعضاء على الاستبيانات التي أجريها الإسكوا. وتهدف هذه الاستبيانات الى تجميع معلومات إضافية تعكس مميزات المنطقة من الأجهزة المركزية للإحصاء.

وفي هذا العدد، أدخلت تعديلات أساسية حيث جرى تحسين نوعية البيانات المنشورة وأهميتها. وكان الهدف من إجراء هذه التغييرات إنتاج أداة أكثر فعالية في رصد البيانات والمؤشرات القابلة للمقارنة.

ويمكن النفاذ الى النسخة الإلكترونية لهذه النشرة على الصفحة الخاصة بإدارة الإحصاء على موقع http://www.escwa.un.org/divisions/main.asp?division=sd.

وتعرب الإسكوا عن شكرها للبلدان الأعضاء لتعاونها في اصدار هذه النشرة.

القسم الأول
Section One

السكان
Population

Section I of this Bulletin, entitled "Population", presents data on population size in the ESCWA region. It is divided into two parts. The first part represents the population estimates[1] and the second part represents the population data from the censuses. This section contains 51 tables and 29 population pyramids for ESCWA member countries.

In this issue, data on all censuses, in the different rounds, conducted in the ESCWA member countries were included. All ESCWA member countries, with the exception of Lebanon, conduct a population census every 10 years. Data have been disaggregated by women, men, national, non-national, urban and rural

Information on the youth and elderly population have been added as well as the dependency ratio.

Population pyramids for all the censuses in the different rounds have been included in this issue. The country pyramids provide a comparative overview of the age distribution for women and men among the member countries.

(1) Data were taken from United Nations Population Division, Department of Economic and Social Affairs (DESA), World Population Prospects: the 2008 revision.

يعرض القسم الأول، المعنون "السكان"، بيانات عن السكان في منطقة الإسكوا. ويضم إلى جزئين: الجزء الأول يشمل التقديرات السكانية(1) والجزء الثاني يعرض بيانات للسكان من التعدادات. ويحتوي هذا القسم على 51 جدول وعلى 29 رسم بياني عن أهرامات السكان في البلدان الأعضاء للإسكوا.

يقدم هذا العدد، بيانات التعدادات التي تم إجراؤها خلال الدورات المختلفة باستثناء لبنان، البلد الوحيد الذي لم يتم إجراء أي تعداد سكاني فيه؛ فإن تقريب جميع بلدان الإسكوا تقوم بتنفيذ التعدادات السكانية كل عشر سنوات. وقد صنفت البيانات حسب رجال ونساء ومواطنين وغير مواطنين وحضر وريف.

تم إضافة معلومات حول الشباب والمسنين ومعدل الإعالة.

تضمن هذا العدد رسومات بيانية للتعدادات (هرم سكاني) التي أجريت خلال الدورات المختلفة والتي تم إضافتها بغرض مقارنة ما بين النساء والرجال حسب التوزيع العمري في بلدان الأعضاء.

(1) استمدت البيانات من آفاق سكان العالم (تنقيح عام 2008) الصادرة عن شعبة السكان بالأمم المتحدة، إدارة الشؤون الاقتصادية والاجتماعية في الأمم المتحدة.

جدول 1: تقديرات السكان في منطقة الإسكوا مقارنة بمناطق اخرى خلال 1990 و1995 و2000 و2005 و2009 (بالألاف)

Table 1: Population estimates in ESCWA Region compared to other region in 1990, 1995, 2000, 2005 and 2009 (in 000s)

COUNTRY	1990	1995	2000	2005	2009	البلد
ESCWA Region [1]	159 445	181 902	206 141	232 278	254 673	منطقة الإسكوا [1]
Arab Region [2]	70 264	78 893	85 411	91 911	97 543	منطقة البلدان العربية [2]
World	5 290 452	5 713 073	6 115 367	6 512 276	6 829 361	العالم
More developed regions [3]	1 147 345	1 174 680	1 194 967	1 216 550	1 233 282	الدول المتقدمة [3]
Less developed regions [4]	3 913 398	4 277 598	4 628 848	4 971 537	5 243 862	الدول النامية [4]

Source: United Nations, World Population Prospects: The 2008 Revision. المصدر: الأمم المتحدة، التوقعات السكانية في العالم: نتيج عام 2008.

(1) ESCWA Region comprises Bahrain, Egypt, Iraq, Jordan, Kuwait, Lebanon, Oman, Palestine, Qatar, Saudi Arabia, Sudan, Syrian Arab Republic, United Arab Emirates and Yemen.

(2) Arab region excludes ESCWA counties and includes only Algeria, Tunisia, Morocco, Mauritania, Libya, Comoros, Somalia, Djibouti,

(3) More developed regions comprise Europe, Northern America, Australia/New Zealand and Japan.

(4) Less developed regions comprise all regions of Africa, Asia (excluding Japan), Latin America and the Caribbean plus Melanesia, Micronesia and Polynesia, excluding Arab & ESCWA Regions

(1) منطقة الإسكوا تشمل البحرين ومصر والعراق والأردن والكويت ولبنان وعمان وفلسطين وقطر والمملكة العربية السعودية والسودان والجمهورية العربية السورية والإمارات العربية المتحدة واليمن.

(2) منطقة البلدان العربية تستثني المنطقة العربية ولبان منطقة الإسكوا وتحتوي على: الجزائر وتونس والمغرب وموريتانيا وليبيا وجزر القمرو وصومالي وجيبوتي فقط.

(3) منطقة الدول المتقدمة تشمل أوربا وأمريكا الشمالية واستراليا ونيوزلاندا واليابان

(4) منطقة الدول النامية تشمل جميع مناطق افريقيا واسيا (باستثناء اليابان) وأمريكا اللاتينية وجزر الكاريبيين وميلانزيا وميكرونيزيا وبولينيزيا باستثناء المنطقة العربية ومنطقة الإسكوا.

Fig. 1: Population estimates of ESCWA region compared to other regions in 2009

شكل 1: تقديرات السكان في منطقة الإسكوا مقارنة بمناطق اخرى في عام 2009

☐ ESCWA Region	منطقة الإسكوا
■ Arab Region	منطقة البلدان العربية
▨ More developed regions	الدول المتقدمة
▨ Less developed regions	الدول النامية

جدول 2: تقديرات السكان (بالألف)، (2009-1990)
Table 2: Population estimates (in 000s), (1990-2009)

COUNTRY	1990	1995	2000	2001	2002	2003	2004	2005	2006	2007	2008	2009	البلد
Bahrain	493	578	650	665	680	696	712	728	744	760	776	791	البحرين
Egypt	57 785	63 858	70 174	71 518	72 894	74 296	75 718	77 154	78 602	80 061	81 527	82 999	مصر
Iraq	18 079	20 971	24 652	25 398	26 137	26 862	27 564	28 238	28 876	29 486	30 096	30 747	العراق
Jordan	3 254	4 304	4 853	4 973	5 103	5 245	5 400	5 566	5 747	5 941	6 136	6 316	الأردن
Kuwait	2 143	1 725	2 228	2 339	2 439	2 531	2 617	2 700	2 779	2 851	2 919	2 985	الكويت
Lebanon	2 974	3 491	3 772	3 833	3 899	3 965	4 028	4 082	4 126	4 162	4 194	4 224	لبنان
Oman	1 843	2 172	2 402	2 443	2 484	2 526	2 570	2 618	2 670	2 726	2 785	2 845	عمان
Palestine	2 154	2 617	3 149	3 266	3 387	3 510	3 636	3 762	3 889	4 017	4 147	4 277	فلسطين
Qatar	467	526	617	648	685	732	797	885	1 001	1 138	1 281	1 409	قطر
Saudi Arabia	16 259	18 255	20 808	21 363	21 927	22 496	23 059	23 613	24 153	24 680	25 201	25 721	المملكة العربية السعودية
Sudan	27 091	30 841	34 904	35 667	36 407	37 142	37 900	38 698	39 545	40 432	41 348	42 272	السودان
Syrian Arab Republic	12 721	14 610	16 511	16 961	17 438	17 952	18 512	19 121	19 789	20 504	21 227	21 906	الجمهورية العربية السورية
United Arab Emirates	1 867	2 432	3 238	3 414	3 591	3 766	3 933	4 089	4 233	4 364	4 485	4 599	الإمارات العربية المتحدة
Yemen	12 314	15 523	18 182	18 722	19 275	19 843	20 426	21 024	21 638	22 269	22 917	23 580	اليمن
ESCWA Region	**159 445**	**181 902**	**206 141**	**211 209**	**216 346**	**221 562**	**226 870**	**232 278**	**237 790**	**243 391**	**249 038**	**254 673**	**منطقة الإسكوا**

Source : United Nations, *World Population Prospects: The 2008 Revision.*

الأمم المتحدة، التوقعات السكانية في العالم، تنقيح عام 2008.

جدول 3: مخزون المهاجرين في بلدان الإسكوا مقارنة بمناطق أخرى، 1990 و 1995 و 2000 و 2005 و 2010
Table 3: International migrant stock in ESCWA countries and other regions, 1990, 1995, 2000, 2005 and 2010

Country	البلد	International migrant stock at mid-year (both sexes) مخزون المهاجرين في منتصف السنة (لكلا الجنسين)				
		1990	1995	2000	2005	2010
Bahrain	البحرين	173 200	205 977	239 366	278 166	315 403
Egypt	مصر	175 574	174 301	169 149	246 745	244 714
Iraq	العراق	83 638	133 733	146 910	128 115	83 380
Jordan	الأردن	1 146 349	1 607 661	1 927 845	2 345 235	2 972 983
Kuwait	الكويت	1 585 280	1 089 545	1 500 442	1 869 665	2 097 527
Lebanon	لبنان	523 693	655 832	692 913	721 191	758 167
Oman	عمان	423 572	582 463	623 608	666 263	826 074
Palestine	فلسطين	910 637	1 200 972	1 407 631	1 660 576	1 923 808
Qatar	قطر	369 816	405 915	470 731	712 861	1 305 428
Saudi Arabia	المملكة العربية السعودية	4 742 997	4 610 694	5 136 402	6 336 666	7 288 900
Sudan	السودان	1 273 141	1 111 143	853 867	639 686	753 447
Syrian Arab Republic	الجمهورية العربية السورية	690 349	816 799	924 086	1 326 359	2 205 847
United Arab Emirates	الإمارات العربية المتحدة	1 330 324	1 715 980	2 286 174	2 863 027	3 293 264
Yemen	اليمن	343 509	377 914	413 530	455 230	517 926
ESCWA Region	**منطقة الإسكوا**	13 772 079	14 688 929	16 792 654	20 249 785	24 586 868
WORLD	**العالم**	155 518 065	165 968 778	178 498 563	195 245 404	213 943 812
More developed regions	**الدول المتقدمة**	82 354 728	94 123 386	104 433 692	117 187 935	127 711 471
Less developed regions	**الدول النامية**	73 163 337	71 845 392	74 064 871	78 057 469	86 232 341
ESCWA Region share of the international migrant stock (%)	**حصة منطقة الإسكوا من مخزون المهاجرين (%)**	8.9	8.9	9.4	10.4	11.5

Source: United Nations Statistics Division, *United Nations Migration Global Database*.

المصدر : شعبة الإحصاء بالأمم المتحدة : قاعدة بيانات الهجرة.

2010-2005 و 2005-2000 و 2000-1995 و 1995-1990 عند الولادة المتوقع العمر :4 جدول

Table 4: Life expectancy at birth, 1990-1995, 1995-2000, 2000-2005 and 2005-2010

العمر المتوقع عند الولادة للجنسين (بالسنوات)

Country	Life expectancy at birth for both sexes combined (years)				البلد
	1990-1995	1995-2000	2000-2005	2005-2010	
Bahrain	72.66	73.91	74.79	75.66	البحرين
Egypt	64.24	67.22	68.96	70.01	مصر
Iraq	66.05	71.14	70.17	67.35	العراق
Jordan	68.02	69.77	71.25	72.53	الأردن
Kuwait	75.19	76.15	76.90	77.59	الكويت
Lebanon	69.29	70.27	71.03	71.99	لبنان
Palestine	69.72	71.10	72.37	73.42	فلسطين
Oman	71.20	72.50	74.19	75.60	عمان
Qatar	69.94	72.01	74.23	75.54	قطر
Saudi Arabia	68.91	70.53	71.63	72.78	المملكة العربية السعودية
Sudan	53.49	55.32	56.71	57.96	السودان
Syrian Arab Republic	69.25	71.53	73.05	74.14	سوريا
United Arab Emirates	73.66	75.88	76.71	77.37	الإمارات العربية المتحدة
Yemen	55.60	58.02	60.31	62.70	اليمن
WORLD	64.01	65.15	66.37	67.58	العالم
More developed regions [1]	74.11	75.00	75.85	77.06	الدول المتقدمة [1]
Less developed regions [2]	61.73	63.06	64.41	65.61	الدول النامية [2]

Source: United Nations, *World Population Prospects: The 2008 Revision.*   المصدر: الأمم المتحدة، التوقعات السكانية في العالم: نتيجة عام 2008.

(1) More developed regions comprise Europe, Northern America, Australia/New Zealand and Japan.

(2) Less developed regions comprise all regions of Africa, Asia (excluding Japan), Latin America and the Caribbean plus Melanesia, Micronesia and Polynesia.

(1) منطقة الدول المتقدمة تشمل اوربا وامريكا الشمالية واستراليا ونيوزيلاندا واليابان

(2) منطقة الدول النامية تشمل جميع مناطق افريقيا، وآسيا (باستثناء اليابان) وامريكا اللاتينية وجزر الكاريبيين وميلانيزيا وميكرونيزيا وبولينيزيا

2010-2005 و 2005-2000 و 2000-1995 و 1995-1990 :نسبة الجنسين عند الولادة: 5 جدول

Table 5: Sex ratio at birth, 1990-1995, 1995-2000, 2000-2005 and 2005-2010

Country	البلد	Sex ratio at birth (male births per female births) (الإناث الولادات على ذكور ولادات) نسبة الجنسين عند الولادة			
		1990-1995	1995-2000	2000-2005	2005-2010
Bahrain	البحرين	1.05	1.05	1.05	1.05
Egypt	مصر	1.05	1.05	1.05	1.05
Iraq	العراق	1.07	1.07	1.07	1.07
Jordan	الاردن	1.05	1.05	1.05	1.05
Kuwait	الكويت	1.03	1.03	1.03	1.03
Lebanon	لبنان	1.05	1.05	1.05	1.05
Palestine	فلسطين	1.05	1.05	1.05	1.05
Oman	عمان	1.05	1.05	1.05	1.05
Qatar	قطر	1.05	1.05	1.05	1.05
Saudi Arabia	المملكة العربية السعودية	1.03	1.03	1.03	1.03
Sudan	السودان	1.05	1.05	1.05	1.05
Syrian Arab Republic	سوريا	1.05	1.05	1.05	1.05
United Arab Emirates	الإمارات العربية المتحدة	1.05	1.05	1.05	1.05
Yemen	اليمن	1.05	1.05	1.05	1.05
WORLD	**العالم**	1.07	1.07	1.07	1.07
More developed regions [1]	**الدول المتقدمة** [1]	1.06	1.06	1.06	1.06
Less developed regions [2]	**الدول النامية** [2]	1.07	1.07	1.08	1.07

Source: United Nations, *World Population Prospects: The 2008 Revision.*   المصدر: الأمم المتحدة، التوقعات السكانية في العالم، تنقيح عام 2008.

(1) More developed regions comprise Europe, Northern America, Australia/New Zealand and Japan.

(1) منطقة الدول المتقدمة تشمل اوروبا واميركا الشمالية واستراليا ونيوزيلندا واليابان.

(2) Less developed regions comprise all regions of Africa, Asia (excluding Japan), Latin America and the Caribbean plus Melanesia, Micronesia and Polynesia.

(2) منطقة الدول النامية تشمل جميع مناطق افريقيا واسيا (باستثناء اليابان) واميركا اللاتينية وجزر الكاريبي وميلانيزيا وميكرونيزيا وبولينيزيا.

-9-

جدول 6: السكان في البحرين بحسب الفئات العمرية، تعداد 1991
Table 6: Population of Bahrain by age groups, 1991 census

الفئة العمرية Age group	المواطنون Nationals		غير مواطنين Non-nationals		حضر Urban		ريف Rural		المجموع Total		
	رجال Men	نساء Women	رجال Men	نساء Women	رجال Men	نساء Women	رجال Men	نساء Women	رجال Men	نساء Women	كلا الجنسين Both sexes
0-4	24 719	23 036	6 242	5 871	...	...	...	...	30 961	28 907	59 868
5-9	22 595	21 498	5 198	4 871	...	...	...	...	27 793	26 369	54 162
10-14	20 373	19 864	3 439	3 146	...	...	...	...	23 812	23 010	46 822
15-19	16 427	15 958	2 234	2 070	...	...	...	...	18 661	18 028	36 689
20-24	14 862	14 705	10 002	6 116	...	...	...	...	24 864	20 821	45 685
25-29	14 550	15 113	22 836	9 399	...	...	...	...	37 386	24 512	61 898
30-34	11 940	13 016	30 211	9 268	...	...	...	...	42 151	22 284	64 435
35-39	9 836	9 236	23 580	6 326	...	...	...	...	33 416	15 562	48 978
40-44	6 880	5 758	13 712	3 382	...	...	...	...	20 592	9 140	29 732
45-49	4 242	4 779	6 865	1 554	...	...	...	...	11 107	6 333	17 440
50-54	4 164	4 717	3 653	868	...	...	...	...	7 817	5 585	13 402
55-59	3 823	3 849	1 684	424	...	...	...	...	5 507	4 273	9 780
60-64	3 431	3 335	733	242	...	...	...	...	4 164	3 577	7 741
65-69	2 427	2 151	245	122	...	...	...	...	2 672	2 273	4 945
70-74	1 613	1 379	119	93	...	...	...	...	1 732	1 472	3 204
75+	1 569	1 458	140	87	...	...	...	...	1 709	1 545	3 254
غير محدد not stated	2	-	-	-	...	...	...	...	2	-	2
المجموع Total	163 453	159 852	130 893	53 839	...	...	...	...	294 346	213 691	508 037

2001 المكان في البحرين بحسب الفئات العمرية، تعداد
Table 7: Population of Bahrain by age groups, 2001 census

الفئة العمرية Age group	المواطنين Nationals		غير مواطنين Non-nationals		حضر Urban		ريف Rural		المجموع Total		
	رجال Men	نساء Women	رجال Men	نساء Women	رجال Men	نساء Women	رجال Men	نساء Women	رجال Men	نساء Women	كلا الجنسين Both sexes
0-4	24 705	23 616	6 249	5 815	:	:	:	:	30 954	29 431	60 385
5-9	25 666	25 059	5 802	5 623	:	:	:	:	31 468	30 682	62 150
10-14	25 281	23 879	5 033	4 641	:	:	:	:	30 314	28 520	58 834
15-19	22 729	21 511	3 603	3 152	:	:	:	:	26 332	24 663	50 995
20-24	19 681	18 677	12 482	7 835	:	:	:	:	32 163	26 512	58 675
25-29	15 303	14 957	27 526	11 589	:	:	:	:	42 829	26 546	69 375
30-34	13 942	14 635	30 823	12 889	:	:	:	:	44 765	27 524	72 289
35-39	14 039	15 298	25 882	10 196	:	:	:	:	39 921	25 494	65 415
40-44	11 816	12 936	23 619	6 887	:	:	:	:	35 435	19 823	55 258
45-49	9 489	8 893	15 522	3 873	:	:	:	:	25 011	12 766	37 777
50-54	6 573	5 468	7 521	1 769	:	:	:	:	14 094	7 237	21 331
55-59	4 198	4 358	2 939	761	:	:	:	:	7 137	5 119	12 256
60-64	3 822	4 172	1 115	392	:	:	:	:	4 937	4 564	9 501
65-69	2 705	3 027	448	221	:	:	:	:	3 153	3 248	6 401
70-74	2 220	2 259	276	124	:	:	:	:	2 496	2 383	4 879
75+	2 454	2 299	186	144	:	:	:	:	2 640	2 443	5083
غير محدد not stated	-	-	-	-	:	:	:	:	-	-	-
المجموع Total	204 623	201 044	169 026	75 911	...	...	...	...	373 649	276 955	650 604

1986 جدول 8: السكان في مصر بحسب الفئات العمرية، تعداد
Table 8: Population of Egypt by age groups, 1986 census

الفئة العمرية Age group	المواطنين Nationals رجال Men	نساء Women	غير مواطنين Non-nationals رجال Men	نساء Women	حضر Urban رجال Men	نساء Women	ريف Rural رجال Men	نساء Women	المجموع Total رجال Men	نساء Women	المجموع كلا الجنسين Both sexes
0-4	:	:	:	:	1 458 625	1 395 486	2 295 223	2 212 847	3 753 848	3 608 333	7 362 181
5-9	:	:	:	:	1 327 312	1 259 960	1 943 346	1 810 468	3 270 658	3 070 428	6 341 086
10-14	:	:	:	:	1 179 588	1 110 666	1 751 050	1 536 616	2 930 638	2 647 282	5 577 920
15-19	:	:	:	:	1 149 162	1 064 767	1 543 736	1 305 967	2 692 898	2 370 734	5 063 632
20-24	:	:	:	:	1 060 122	990 776	1 162 550	1 034 093	2 222 672	2 024 869	4 247 541
25-29	:	:	:	:	843 485	893 364	944 958	1 015 701	1 788 443	1 909 065	3 697 508
30-34	:	:	:	:	767 820	760 342	746 790	770 372	1 514 610	1 530 714	3 045 324
35-39	:	:	:	:	725 201	672 529	766 550	761 026	1 491 751	1 433 555	2 925 306
40-44	:	:	:	:	537 097	496 616	517 840	576 399	1 054 937	1 073 015	2 127 952
45-49	:	:	:	:	456 232	411 282	516 252	531 474	972 484	942 756	1 915 240
50-54	:	:	:	:	389 691	397 457	406 447	502 081	796 138	899 538	1 695 676
55-59	:	:	:	:	308 788	248 468	364 349	330 689	673 137	579 157	1 252 294
60-64	:	:	:	:	261 470	246 296	292 540	330 907	554 010	577 203	1 131 213
65-69	:	:	:	:	160 744	122 127	191 520	208 100	352 264	330 227	682 491
70-74	:	:	:	:	118 247	94 207	175 061	142 601	293 308	236 808	530 116
75+	:	:	:	:	85 403	80 470	109 634	110 410	195 037	190 880	385 917
غير محدد not stated	:	:	:	:	79 862	61 841	72 578	58 559	152 440	120 400	272 840
المجموع Total	...	...	...	...	10 908 849	10 306 654	13 800 424	13 238 310	24 709 273	23 544 964	43 254 237

جدول 9: السكان في مصر بحسب الفئات العمرية، تعداد 1996

Table 9: Population of Egypt by age groups, 1996 census

القئة العمرية Age group	Nationals المواطنين		Non-nationals غير مواطنين		Urban حضر		Rural ريف		Total		المجموع كلا الجنسين Both sexes
	رجال Men	نساء Women	رجال Men	نساء Women	رجال Men	نساء Women	رجال Men	نساء Women	رجال Men	نساء Women	
0-4	...	...	...	...	1 274 892	1 221 449	2 236 884	2 122 017	3 511 776	3 343 466	6 855 242
5-9	...	...	...	...	1 464 520	1 387 698	2 474 601	2 299 433	3 939 121	3 687 131	7 626 252
10-14	...	...	...	...	1 602 009	1 514 199	2 474 592	2 273 202	4 076 601	3 787 401	7 864 002
15-19	...	...	...	...	1 510 230	1 420 081	2 092 627	1 878 673	3 602 857	3 298 754	6 901 611
20-24	...	...	...	...	1 167 895	1 105 656	1 474 725	1 326 860	2 642 620	2 432 516	5 075 136
25-29	...	...	...	...	933 765	982 469	1 171 298	1 282 990	2 105 063	2 265 459	4 370 522
30-34	...	...	...	...	917 762	929 346	1 075 450	1 057 162	1 993 212	1 986 508	3 979 720
35-39	...	...	...	...	879 215	896 879	1 035 152	1 048 859	1 914 367	1 945 738	3 860 105
40-44	...	...	...	...	810 931	763 029	805 518	793 748	1 616 449	1 556 777	3 173 226
45-49	...	...	...	...	687 877	609 035	720 621	678 636	1 408 498	1 287 671	2 696 169
50-54	...	...	...	...	503 584	481 233	491 352	545 967	994 936	1 027 200	2 022 136
55-59	...	...	...	...	372 516	313 625	404 021	386 511	776 537	700 136	1 476 673
60-64	...	...	...	...	349 766	315 675	356 423	377 130	706 189	692 805	1 398 994
65-69	...	...	...	...	232 503	172 142	274 582	251 349	507 085	423 491	930 576
70-74	...	...	...	...	144 153	124 912	171 614	176 990	315 767	301 902	617 669
75+	...	...	...	...	106 154	91 128	134 148	133 428	240 302	224 556	464 858
غير محدد not stated	...	...	...	...	3	4	7	9	10	13	23
المجموع Total	...	...	...	...	12 957 775	12 328 560	17 393 615	16 632 964	30 351 390	28 961 524	59 312 914

2006 جدول 10: السكان في مصر بحسب الفئات العمرية، تعداد
Table 10: Population of Egypt by age groups, 2006 census

الفئة العمرية Age group	المواطنين Nationals		غير مواطنين Non-nationals		حضر Urban		ريف Rural		المجموع Total		كلا الجنسين Both sexes
	رجال Men	نساء Women	رجال Men	نساء Women	رجال Men	نساء Women	رجال Men	نساء Women	رجال Men	نساء Women	المجموع Both sexes
0-4	4 231 397	4 024 007	4 214	3 850	...	...	...	...	4 235 611	4 027 857	8 263 468
5-9	4 744 139	4 437 825	4 427	4 012	...	...	...	...	4 748 566	4 441 837	9 190 403
10-14	4 908 718	4 559 117	4 574	4 338	...	...	...	...	4 913 292	4 563 455	9 476 747
15-19	4 344 315	3 975 933	5 759	4 740	...	...	...	...	4 350 074	3 980 673	8 330 747
20-24	3 175 297	2 903 359	8 978	6 143	...	...	...	...	3 184 275	2 909 502	6 093 777
25-29	2 517 666	2 731 447	6 517	5 337	...	...	...	...	2 524 183	2 736 784	5 260 967
30-34	2 405 265	2 419 374	6 218	5 351	...	...	...	...	2 411 483	2 424 725	4 836 208
35-39	2 297 883	2 317 903	5 030	4 175	...	...	...	...	2 302 913	2 322 078	4 624 991
40-44	1 932 096	1 889 329	4 896	3 602	...	...	...	...	1 936 992	1 892 931	3 829 923
45-49	1 675 757	1 539 636	3 810	2 712	...	...	...	...	1 679 567	1 542 348	3 221 915
50-54	1 202 176	1 225 326	3 567	2296	...	...	...	...	1 205 743	1 227 622	2 433 365
55-59	947 728	839 476	2 322	1495	...	...	...	...	950 050	840 971	1 791 021
60-64	845 859	832 166	1814	1332	...	...	...	...	847 673	833 498	1 681 171
65-69	611359	508973			...	...	...	...			
70-74	377 776	357 159	2242	1943	...	...	...	...	1 282 545	1 146 107	2 428 652
75+	291 168	278 032			...	...	...	...			
غير محدد not stated	...	...	...	...	...	...	...	...	...	...	...
المجموع Total	36 508 599	34 839 062	64 368	51 326	...	...	...	...	36 572 967	34 890 388	71 463 355

جدول 11: السكان في العراق بحسب الفئات العمرية، تعداد 1987

Table 11: Population of Iraq by age groups, 1987 census

الفئة العمرية Age group	المواطنون Nationals رجال Men	نساء Women	غير مواطنين Non-nationals رجال Men	نساء Women	حضر Urban رجال Men	نساء Women	ريف Rural رجال Men	نساء Women	Total رجال Men	نساء Women	كلا الجنسين المجموع Both sexes
0-4	...	...	...	...	942 152	901 738	473 924	447 019	1 416 076	1 348 757	2 764 833
5-9	...	...	...	...	849 732	816 617	410 102	391 799	1 259 834	1 208 416	2 468 250
10-14	...	...	...	...	757 781	719 771	344 475	326 382	1 102 256	1 046 153	2 148 409
15-19	...	...	...	...	692 777	636 128	304 010	276 196	996 787	912 324	1 909 111
20-24	...	...	...	...	610 758	510 354	195 354	197 556	806 112	707 910	1 514 022
25-29	...	...	...	...	438 268	364 154	92 971	122 988	531 239	487 142	1 018 381
30-34	...	...	...	...	399 508	348 959	131 602	138 619	531 110	487 578	1 018 688
35-39	...	...	...	...	276 002	257 569	96 295	111 461	372 297	369 030	741 327
40-44	...	...	...	...	223 758	189 656	73 305	74 096	297 063	263 752	560 815
45-49	...	...	...	...	185 678	155 255	60 290	55 966	245 968	211 221	457 189
50-54	...	...	...	...	124 782	122 564	42 891	46 977	167 673	169 541	337 214
55-59	...	...	...	...	126 161	127 725	49 926	52 156	176 087	179 881	355 968
60-64	...	...	...	...	81 830	100 557	38 650	46 509	120 480	147 066	267 546
65-69	...	...	...	...	57 009	65 488	32 266	32 717	89 275	98 205	187 480
70-74	...	...	...	...	48 946	53 784	28 313	26 272	77 259	80 056	157 315
75+	...	...	...	...	65 814	79 192	37 482	39 374	103 296	118 566	221 862
غير محدد not stated	...	...	...	...	70 447	68 055	32 630	35 657	103 077	103 712	206 789
المجموع Total	...	...	...	...	5 951 403	5 517 566	2 444 486	2 421 744	8 395 889	7 939 310	16 335 199

جدول 12: السكان في العراق بحسب الفئات العمرية، تعداد 1997
Table 12: Population of Iraq by age groups, 1997 census

القئة العمرية / Age group	المواطنين / Nationals		غير مواطنين / Non-nationals		حضر / Urban		ريف / Rural		المجموع / Total		كلا الجنسين / Both sexes
	رجال / Men	نساء / Women	رجال / Men	نساء / Women	رجال / Men	نساء / Women	رجال / Men	نساء / Women	رجال / Men	نساء / Women	
0-4	:	:	:	:	1 218 197	1 188 647	693 650	678 488	1 911 847	1 867 135	3 778 982
5-9	:	:	:	:	1 124 600	1 087 118	567 526	544 208	1 692 126	1 631 326	3 323 452
10-14	:	:	:	:	955 442	918 804	469 604	448 068	1 425 046	1 366 872	2 791 918
15-19	:	:	:	:	883 604	846 938	409 832	399 830	1 293 436	1 246 768	2 540 204
20-24	:	:	:	:	713 054	706 362	306 213	322 115	1 019 267	1 028 477	2 047 744
25-29	:	:	:	:	591 288	606 625	258 096	268 456	849 384	875 081	1 724 465
30-34	:	:	:	:	499 004	509 079	181 806	201 197	680 810	710 276	1 391 086
35-39	:	:	:	:	327 146	359 495	86 760	126 752	413 906	486 247	900 153
40-44	:	:	:	:	316 790	323 836	112 632	130 766	429 422	454 602	884 024
45-49	:	:	:	:	239 218	244 225	88 217	106 065	327 435	350 290	677 725
50-54	:	:	:	:	197 065	184 976	66 790	71 642	263 855	256 618	520 473
55-59	:	:	:	:	162 203	153 921	52 862	55 215	215 065	209 136	424 201
60-64	:	:	:	:	99 247	113 184	35 597	43 538	134 844	156 722	291 566
65-69	:	:	:	:	86 028	103 180	37 398	43 858	123 426	147 038	270 464
70-74	:	:	:	:	53 298	75 045	28 715	36 055	82 013	111 100	193 113
75+	:	:	:	:	76 326	105 103	49 043	56 202	125 369	161 305	286 674
غير محدد / not stated	:	:	:	:	-	-	-	-	-	-	-
المجموع / Total	:	:	:	:	7 542 510	7 526 538	3 444 741	3 532 455	10 987 251	11 058 993	22 046 244

-16-

جدول 13: السكان في الأردن بحسب الفئات العمرية، تعداد 1994
Table 13: Population of Jordan by age groups, 1994 census

القئة العمرية Age group	المواطنون Nationals		غير مواطنين Non-nationals		حضر Urban		ريف Rural		Total		كلا الجنسين المجموع
	رجال Men	نساء Women	رجال Men	نساء Women	رجال Men	نساء Women	رجال Men	نساء Women	رجال Men	نساء Women	Both sexes
0-4	316 307	300 609	16 375	15 510	242 933	230 782	73 374	69 854	332 682	316 119	648 801
5-9	289 767	276 639	13 289	12 914	220987	211628	68 780	65 011	303 056	289 553	592 609
10-14	271 179	257 880	11 285	10 322	207860	198604	63 319	59 276	282 464	268 202	550 666
15-19	251 160	232 388	17 175	10 464	194129	180378	57 031	52 010	268 335	242 852	511 187
20-24	243 622	209 801	35 291	12 762	191806	166094	51 816	43 707	278 913	222 563	501 476
25-29	209 365	169 587	44 406	11 504	166150	136017	43 215	33 570	253 771	181 091	434 862
30-34	145 584	126 792	27 717	9 242	117967	103144	27 617	23 648	173 301	136 034	309 335
35-39	98 364	90 146	15 322	6 660	79303	72849	19 061	17 297	113 686	96 806	210 492
40-44	73 128	68 012	10 420	4 840	57507	54366	15 621	13 646	83 548	72 852	156 400
45-49	63 161	64 239	6 570	3 607	51162	52235	11 999	12 004	69 731	67 846	137 577
50-54	61 149	53 169	4 350	2 480	49729	42777	11 420	10 392	65 499	55 649	121 148
55-59	48 299	43 322	2 521	1 699	38940	34671	9 359	8 651	50 820	45 021	95 841
60-64	35 251	32 754	1 585	1 409	27704	25845	7 547	6 909	36 836	34 163	70 999
65-69	22 799	19 433	877	841	18037	15760	4 762	3 673	23 676	20 274	43 950
70-74	13 621	15 997	531	711	10222	12250	3 399	3 747	14 152	16 708	30 860
75+	15 835	16 448	447	676	11450	12745	4 385	3 703	16 282	17 124	33 406
غير محدد not stated	2 134	1 517	907	256	1 644	1 082	490	435	3 041	1 773	4 814
المجموع Total	2 160 725	1 978 733	209 068	105 897	1 687 530	1 551 227	473 195	427 533	2 369 793	2 084 630	4 454 423

2004 جدول 14: السكان في الأردن بحسب الفئات العمرية، تعداد
Table 14: Population of Jordan by age groups, 2004 census

الفئة العمرية Age group	المواطنين Nationals		غير مواطنين Non-nationals		حضر Urban		ريف Rural		المجموع Total		
	رجال Men	نساء Women	رجال Men	نساء Women	رجال Men	نساء Women	رجال Men	نساء Women	رجال Men	نساء Women	كلا الجنسين Both sexes
0-4	314 778	299 417	18 438	17 698	257 669	246 198	75 547	70 917	333 216	317 115	650 331
5-9	313 300	298 550	15 833	15 188	253 774	241 809	75 359	71 929	329 133	313 738	642 871
10-14	298 669	283 693	14 414	13 353	240 723	228 598	72 360	68 448	313 083	297 046	610 129
15-19	270 699	257 522	16 994	14 623	221 213	210 062	66 480	62 083	287 693	272 145	559 838
20-24	248 508	232 933	31 092	27 660	217 092	204 308	62 508	56 285	279 600	260 593	540 193
25-29	202 463	193 959	37 311	22 528	186 570	169 380	53 204	47 107	239 774	216 487	456 261
30-34	174 537	175 223	32 641	16 768	164 238	151 997	42 940	39 994	207 178	191 991	399 169
35-39	145 100	145 613	22 637	10 076	134 829	124 907	32 908	30 782	167 737	155 689	323 426
40-44	108 609	111 054	15 336	6 401	101 442	95 481	22 503	21 974	123 945	117 455	241 400
45-49	78 163	79 165	8 935	4 193	70 890	67 482	16 208	15 876	87 098	83 358	170 456
50-54	58 488	60 234	6 119	3 399	51 210	50 969	13 397	12 664	64 607	63 633	128 240
55-59	51 589	55 163	4 176	2 793	45 618	47 275	10 147	10 681	55 765	57 956	113 721
60-64	49 252	44 722	2 832	1 981	42 634	37 635	9 450	9 068	52 084	46 703	98 787
65-69	35 497	33 430	1 598	1 298	29 956	27 528	7 139	7 200	37 095	34 728	71 823
70-74	22 574	22 447	893	906	18 503	18 455	4 964	4 898	23 467	23 353	46 820
75+	22 059	22 631	729	909	17 292	18 244	5 496	5 296	22 788	23 540	46328
غير محدد not stated	662	663	1362	1159	1778	1624	246	198	2024	1822	3846
المجموع Total	2 394 947	2 316 419	231 340	160 933	2 055 431	1 941 952	570 856	535 400	2 626 287	2 477 352	5 103 639

جدول 15: السكان في الكويت بحسب الفئات العمرية، تعداد 1985
Table 15: Population of Kuwait by age groups, 1985 census

الفئة العمرية Age group	Nationals رجال Men	نساء Women	Non-nationals رجال Men	نساء Women	Urban رجال Men	نساء Women	Rural رجال Men	ريف نساء Women	Total رجال Men	نساء Women	المجموع كلا الجنسين Both sexes
0-4	42 247	41 288	81 010	77 655	…	…	…	…	123 257	118 943	242 200
5-9	37 014	36 255	70 077	67 041	…	…	…	…	107 091	103 296	210 387
10-14	32 264	31 653	55 600	52 981	…	…	…	…	87 864	84 634	172 498
15-19	27 820	26 375	45 615	46 124	…	…	…	…	73 435	72 499	145 934
20-24	22 293	22 063	54 607	49 425	…	…	…	…	76 900	71 488	148 388
25-29	16 893	18 408	98 102	53 853	…	…	…	…	114 995	72 261	187 256
30-34	12 654	14 350	98 323	48 396	…	…	…	…	110 977	62 746	173 723
35-39	9 198	11 383	79 268	37 712	…	…	…	…	88 466	49 095	137 561
40-44	8 578	8 887	56 230	24 385	…	…	…	…	64 808	33 272	98 080
45-49	8 731	6 932	40 127	16 558	…	…	…	…	48 858	23 490	72 348
50-54	6 478	4 999	24 890	9 857	…	…	…	…	31 368	14 856	46 224
55-59	8 114	3 376	13 123	5 710	…	…	…	…	21 237	9 086	30 323
60-64	3 460	2 434	5 580	3 697	…	…	…	…	9 040	6 131	15 171
65+	6 175	3 889	4 474	3 318	…	…	…	…	10 649	7 207	17 856
غير محدد not stated	-	-	-	-	…	…	…	…	-	-	-
المجموع Total	241 919	232 292	727 026	496 712	…	…	…	…	968 945	729 004	1 697 949

جدول 16: السكان في الكويت بحسب الفئات العمرية، تعداد 1995

Table 16: Population of Kuwait by age groups, 1995 census

القئة العمرية Age group	المواطنين Nationals رجال Men	نساء Women	غير مواطنين Non-nationals رجال Men	نساء Women	حضر Urban رجال Men	نساء Women	ريف Rural رجال Men	نساء Women	المجموع Total رجال Men	نساء Women	كلا الجنسين Both sexes
0-4	55 281	52 075	31 236	29 573	...	...	...	...	86 517	81 648	168 165
5-9	49 883	48 300	33 925	31 896	...	...	...	...	83 808	80 196	164 004
10-14	42 751	41 257	28 316	27 003	...	...	...	...	71 067	68 260	139 327
15-19	35 916	35 256	20 078	19 342	...	...	...	...	55 994	54 598	110 592
20-24	30 692	29 879	38 602	33 972	...	...	...	...	69 294	63 851	133 145
25-29	25 893	25 415	99 389	52 606	...	...	...	...	125 282	78 021	203 303
30-34	20 997	21 503	103 567	49 543	...	...	...	...	124 564	71 046	195 610
35-39	15 758	18 620	88 677	38 976	...	...	...	...	104 435	57 596	162 031
40-44	12 039	14 896	62 695	23 587	...	...	...	...	74 734	38 483	113 217
45-49	8 499	11 875	38 909	12 360	...	...	...	...	47 408	24 235	71 643
50-54	7 684	8 993	20 918	6166	...	...	...	...	28 602	15 159	43 761
55-59	7 300	6 887	11 996	3574	...	...	...	...	19 296	10 461	29 757
60-64	4 844	4 658	4682	2123	...	...	...	...	9 526	6 781	16 307
65-69	7 892	6 883	2996	2884	...	...	...	...	10 888	9 767	20 655
70+	872 000	818 000	1115	1248	...	...	...	...	873 115	819 248	1 692 363
غير محدد not stated	-	-	-	-	...	...	...	...	-	-	-
المجموع Total	1 197 429	1 144 497	587 101	334 853	...	...	...	...	1 784 530	1 479 350	3 263 880

جدول 17: السكان في الكويت بحسب الفئات العمرية، تعداد 2005
Table 17: Population of Kuwait by age groups, 2005 census

القئة العمرية Age group	المواطنون Nationals رجال Men	نساء Women	غير مواطنين Non-nationals رجال Men	نساء Women	حضر Urban رجال Men	نساء Women	ريف Rural رجال Men	نساء Women	المجموع Total رجال Men	نساء Women	كلا الجنسين Both sexes
0-4	59 349	55 874	40 116	36 836	⋮	⋮	⋮	⋮	99 465	92 710	192 175
5-9	60 713	56 447	36 483	34 362	⋮	⋮	⋮	⋮	97 196	90 809	188 005
10-14	56 307	52 961	30 358	27 262	⋮	⋮	⋮	⋮	86 665	80 223	166 888
15-19	49 908	48 294	30 820	27 027	⋮	⋮	⋮	⋮	80 728	75 321	156 049
20-24	40 363	39 596	73 278	46 927	⋮	⋮	⋮	⋮	113 641	86 523	200 164
25-29	31 017	33 425	144 668	71 197	⋮	⋮	⋮	⋮	175 685	104 622	280 307
30-34	27 294	30 291	145 039	66 849	⋮	⋮	⋮	⋮	172 333	97 140	269 473
35-39	24 481	27 565	130 143	55 678	⋮	⋮	⋮	⋮	154 624	83 243	237 867
40-44	20 827	23 616	94 116	39 253	⋮	⋮	⋮	⋮	114 943	62 869	177 812
45-49	15 727	19 912	68 968	24 309	⋮	⋮	⋮	⋮	84 695	44 221	128 916
50-54	11 827	15 144	42 088	13 175	⋮	⋮	⋮	⋮	53 915	28 319	82 234
55-59	8 120	11 328	22 165	6941	⋮	⋮	⋮	⋮	30 285	18 269	48 554
60-64	6 834	8 134	9 652	3714	⋮	⋮	⋮	⋮	16 486	11 848	28 334
65+	12 458	12 458	7174	4729	⋮	⋮	⋮	⋮	19 632	17 187	36 819
غير محدد not stated	-	-	-	-					-	-	-
المجموع Total	425 225	435 045	875 068	458 259	…	…	…	…	1 300 293	893 304	2 193 597

1993 جدول 18: السكان في عمان بحسب الفئات العمرية، تعداد
Table 18: Population of Oman by age groups, 1993 census

الفئة العمرية Age group	Nationals رجال Men	المواطنات Women	Non-nationals رجال Men	غير مواطنين Women	Urban رجال Men	حضر Women	Rural رجال Men	ريف Women	Total رجال Men	نساء Women	كلا الجنسين Both sexes
0-4	130 207	125 408	12 737	12 532	95 163	91 547	47 781	46 393	142 944	137 940	280 884
5-9	136 263	132 395	11 647	11 212	99 506	96 043	48 404	47 564	147 910	143 607	291 517
10-14	122 959	117 889	7 167	6 796	88 511	85 073	41 615	39 612	130 126	124 685	254 811
15-19	90 319	84 990	3 400	2 969	67 343	61 960	26 376	25 999	93 719	87 959	181 678
20-24	57 920	52 490	28 810	9 831	64 794	46 278	21 936	16 043	86 730	62 321	149 051
25-29	40 642	40 139	83 977	19 916	97 490	46 162	27 129	13 893	124 619	60 055	184 674
30-34	31 989	33 108	92 453	19 940	99 200	41 045	25 242	12 003	124 442	53 048	177 490
35-39	28 297	32 406	81 631	13 991	88 582	34 587	21 346	11 810	109 928	46 397	156 325
40-44	23 324	23 576	53 586	7 413	61 573	22 270	15 337	8 719	76 910	30 989	107 899
45-49	21 330	20 965	27 308	3 493	37 502	16 644	11 136	7 814	48 638	24 458	73 096
50-54	21 107	19 549	12 834	1612	24 562	13 878	9 379	7 283	33 941	21 161	55 102
55-59	13 439	11 003	4 371	823	12 398	7 812	5 412	4 014	17 810	11 826	29 636
60-64	14 949	12 124	1623	567	10 262	7 978	6 310	4 713	16 572	12 691	29 263
65-69	6 857	5 921	421	304	4 477	3 967	2 801	2 258	7 278	6 225	13 503
70-74	6 952	7 211	223	190	4 173	4 440	3 002	2 961	7 175	7 401	14 576
75+	8 403	8 855	186	178	4 909	5 447	3 680	3 586	8 589	9 033	17 622
غير محدد not stated	153	87	521	186	540	242	134	31	674	273	947
المجموع Total	755 110	728 116	422 895	111 953	860 985	585 373	317 020	254 696	1 178 005	840 069	2 018 074

جدول 19: السكان في عمان بحسب الفئات العمرية، تعداد 2003
Table 19: Population of Oman by age groups, 2003 census

الفئة العمرية Age group	المواطنون Nationals		غير مواطنين Non-nationals		حضر Urban		ريف Rural		المجموع Total		
	رجال Men	نساء Women	رجال Men	نساء Women	رجال Men	نساء Women	رجال Men	نساء Women	رجال Men	نساء Women	كلا الجنسين Both sexes
0-4	109 543	105 986	13 829	13 399	83 774	80 886	39 598	38 499	123 372	119 385	242 757
5-9	121 220	116 256	12 137	11 309	88 659	84 180	44 698	43 385	133 357	127 565	260 922
10-14	137 621	132 644	9 620	8 335	97 801	93 422	49 440	47 557	147 241	140 979	288 220
15-19	130 466	124 741	6 082	5 467	93 894	87 920	42 654	42 288	136 548	130 208	266 756
20-24	107 482	106 778	23 493	15 013	96 847	89 323	34 128	32 468	130 975	121 791	252 766
25-29	74 032	74 227	64 195	23 027	105 365	74 232	32 862	23 022	138 227	97 254	235 481
30-34	47 499	45 276	77 107	23 989	97 306	54 689	27 300	14 576	124 606	69 265	193 871
35-39	35 741	37 347	68 399	18 972	81 623	43 348	22 517	12 971	104 140	56 319	160 459
40-44	29 449	31 527	59 122	12 511	69 905	33 050	18 666	10 988	88 571	44 038	132 609
45-49	23 715	26 839	40 523	6 626	50 116	24 188	14 122	9 277	64 238	33 465	97 703
50-54	20 383	22 312	23 406	3 535	33 611	17 967	10 178	7 880	43 789	25 847	69 636
55-59	15 935	15 203	8 707	1732	17 948	11 508	6 694	5 427	24 642	16 935	41 577
60-64	17 240	14 808	3 485	1067	13 643	10 350	7 082	5 525	20 725	15 875	36 600
65-69	10 389	7 989	1074	617	7 315	5 571	4 148	3 035	11 463	8 606	20 069
70-74	8 959	7 973	588	413	5 815	5 257	3 732	3 129	9 547	8 386	17 933
75+	10 654	10 949	507	419	6 424	6 941	4 737	4 427	11 161	11 368	22 529
غير محدد not stated	212	163	425	127	425	177	212	113	637	290	927
المجموع Total	900 540	881 018	412 699	146 558	950 471	723 009	362 768	304 567	1 313 239	1 027 576	2 340 815

جدول 20: السكان في فلسطين بحسب الفئات العمرية تعداد 1997 (1)

Table 20: Population of Palestine by age groups, 1997 census (1)

القئة العمرية / Age group	المواطنون / Nationals رجال / Men	نساء / Women	غير مواطنين / Non-nationals رجال / Men	نساء / Women	حضر / Urban رجال / Men	نساء / Women	ريف / Rural رجال / Men	نساء / Women	المجموع / Total رجال / Men	نساء / Women	كلا الجنسين / Both sexes
0-4	245 122	233 541	53	56	...	...	...	...	245 175	233 597	478 772
5-9	216 547	206 207	52	45	...	...	...	...	216 599	206 252	422 851
10-14	165 224	156 222	71	56	...	...	...	...	165 295	156 278	321 573
15-19	140 675	132 372	72	232	...	...	...	...	140 747	132 604	273 351
20-24	122 181	113 814	136	525	...	...	...	...	122 317	114 339	236 656
25-29	98 766	91 456	196	485	...	...	...	...	98 962	91 941	190 903
30-34	86 044	78 840	151	328	...	...	...	...	86 195	79 168	165 363
35-39	64 317	59 112	108	233	...	...	...	...	64 425	59 345	123 770
40-44	44 303	44 046	81	238	...	...	...	...	44 384	44 284	88 668
45-49	34 793	33 307	87	164	...	...	...	...	34 880	33 471	68 351
50-54	26 018	29 800	73	107	...	...	...	...	26 091	29 907	55 998
55-59	17 545	24 314	53	72	...	...	...	...	17 598	24 386	41 984
60-64	18 741	23 053	45	64	...	...	...	...	18 786	23 117	41 903
65-69	14 728	19 652	27	42	...	...	...	...	14 755	19 694	34 449
70-74	10 925	13 971	16	36	...	...	...	...	10 941	14 007	24 948
75+	14 364	16 376	25	57	...	...	...	...	14 389	16 433	30 822
غير مبين / not stated	695	545	30	37	...	...	...	...	725	582	1 307
المجموع / Total	1 320 988	1 276 628	1 276	2 777	...	...	...	...	1 322 264	1 279 405	2 601 669

(1) Data don't include that part of Jerusalem which was annexed forcefully by Israel in 1967.

(1) البيانات لا تشمل ذلك الجزء من محافظة القدس الذي ضمته إسرائيل عنوة بعد احتلالها للضفة الغربية عام 1967.

جدول 21: السكان في فلسطين بحسب الفئات العمرية، تعداد 2007 (1)
Table 21: Population of Palestine by age groups, 2007 census (1)

القئة العمرية Age group	المواطنين Nationals رجال Men	نساء Women	غير مواطنين Non-nationals رجال Men	نساء Women	حضر Urban رجال Men	نساء Women	ريف Rural رجال Men	نساء Women	المجموع Total رجال Men	نساء Women	كلا الجنسين Both sexes
0-4	: :	: :	: :	: :	: :	: :	: :	: :	302 905	290 544	593 449
5-9	: :	: :	: :	: :	: :	: :	: :	: :	276 802	265 674	542 476
10-14	: :	: :	: :	: :	: :	: :	: :	: :	254 693	244 299	498 992
15-19	: :	: :	: :	: :	: :	: :	: :	: :	219 408	210 992	430 400
20-24	: :	: :	: :	: :	: :	: :	: :	: :	169 381	160 787	330 168
25-29	: :	: :	: :	: :	: :	: :	: :	: :	138 971	134 482	273 453
30-34	: :	: :	: :	: :	: :	: :	: :	: :	117 446	115 277	232 723
35-39	: :	: :	: :	: :	: :	: :	: :	: :	98 469	94 780	193 249
40-44	: :	: :	: :	: :	: :	: :	: :	: :	87 006	80 511	167 517
45-49	: :	: :	: :	: :	: :	: :	: :	: :	66 646	61 472	128 118
50-54	: :	: :	: :	: :	: :	: :	: :	: :	45 578	44 473	90 051
55-59	: :	: :	: :	: :	: :	: :	: :	: :	33 761	32 836	66 597
60-64	: :	: :	: :	: :	: :	: :	: :	: :	23 554	27 545	51 099
65-69	: :	: :	: :	: :	: :	: :	: :	: :	15 997	21 505	37 502
70-74	: :	: :	: :	: :	: :	: :	: :	: :	13 653	17 763	31 416
75+	: :	: :	: :	: :	: :	: :	: :	: :	18 314	24 872	43 186
غير محدد not stated	: :	: :	: :	: :	: :	: :	: :	: :	29 372	27 357	56 729
المجموع Total	....	....	....	....	....	....	....	....	1 911 956	1 855 169	3 767 125

(1) Incldues population counted during the period 1-16 December 2007 and uncounted population estimates according to post enumration survey.

(1) يشمل السكان الذين تم عدهم خلال الفترة 16-1 كانون الأول/ديسمبر 2007 وتقديرات السكان الذين تم عدهم، وفقا للاستقصاء اللاحق لعملية العد.

جدول 22: السكان في قطر بحسب الفئات العمرية، تعداد 1986

Table 22: Population of Qatar by age groups, 1986 census

الفئة العمرية Age group	المواطنين Nationals		غير مواطنين Non-nationals		حضر Urban		ريف Rural		المجموع Total		الجنسين Both sexes
	رجال Men	نساء Women	رجال Men	نساء Women	رجال Men	نساء Women	رجال Men	نساء Women	رجال Men	نساء Women	
0-4	...	...	...	...	...	...	...	...	20 965	20 189	41 154
5-9	...	...	...	...	...	...	...	...	17 774	16 870	34 644
10-14	...	...	...	...	...	...	...	...	13 871	12 783	26 654
15-19	...	...	...	...	...	...	...	...	12 338	10 295	22 633
20-24	...	...	...	...	...	...	...	...	22 121	10 448	32 569
25-29	...	...	...	...	...	...	...	...	41 664	11 530	53 194
30-34	...	...	...	...	...	...	...	...	41 004	13 248	54 252
35-39	...	...	...	...	...	...	...	...	30 158	9 826	39 984
40-44	...	...	...	...	...	...	...	...	19 236	5 845	25 081
45-49	...	...	...	...	...	...	...	...	12 742	3 721	16 463
50-54	...	...	...	...	...	...	...	...	7 692	2 458	10 150
55-59	...	...	...	...	...	...	...	...	3 848	1 388	5 236
60-64	...	...	...	...	...	...	...	...	2 177	1 025	3 202
65-69	...	...	...	...	...	...	...	...	1 003	0 577	1 580
70-74	...	...	...	...	...	...	...	...	565	467	1032
75+	...	...	...	...	...	...	...	...	621	537	1158
غير محدد not stated	...	...	...	...	...	...	...	...	73	20	93
المجموع Total	...	...	...	...	...	...	...	...	247 852	121 227	369 079

جدول 23: السكان في قطر بحسب الفئات العمرية، تعداد 2004
Table 23: Population of Qatar by age groups, 2004 census

القئة العمرية Age group	المواطنين Nationals		غير مواطنين Non-nationals		حضر Urban		ريف Rural		المجموع Total		
	رجال Men	نساء Women	رجال Men	نساء Women	رجال Men	نساء Women	رجال Men	نساء Women	رجال Men	نساء Women	كلا الجنسين Both sexes
0-4	:	:	:	:	:	:	:	:	30 059	28 489	58 548
5-9	:	:	:	:	:	:	:	:	28 420	27 814	56 234
10-14	:	:	:	:	:	:	:	:	26 687	26 149	52 836
15-19	:	:	:	:	:	:	:	:	22 187	20 004	42 191
20-24	:	:	:	:	:	:	:	:	39 896	19 671	59 567
25-29	:	:	:	:	:	:	:	:	59 477	24 576	84 053
30-34	:	:	:	:	:	:	:	:	66 976	27 833	94 809
35-39	:	:	:	:	:	:	:	:	61 624	23 773	85 397
40-44	:	:	:	:	:	:	:	:	56 617	19 260	75 877
45-49	:	:	:	:	:	:	:	:	46 488	12 631	59 119
50-54	:	:	:	:	:	:	:	:	29 738	7 615	37 353
55-59	:	:	:	:	:	:	:	:	15 771	4 104	19 875
60-64	:	:	:	:	:	:	:	:	6 768	2 359	9 127
65-69	:	:	:	:	:	:	:	:	2 805	1 504	4 309
70-74	:	:	:	:	:	:	:	:	1 619	0 925	2 544
75+	:	:	:	:	:	:	:	:	1 250	0 940	2190
غير محدد not stated	:	:	:	:	:	:	:	:	-	-	-
المجموع Total	...	...	...	...	...	...	...	...	496 382	247 647	744 029

1992 تعداد السكان في المملكة العربية السعودية بحسب الفئات العمرية **:24 جدول**

Table 24: Population of Saudi Arabia by age groups, 1992 census

القئة العمرية Age group	النواطنين Nationals		غير مواطنين Non-nationals		حضر Urban		ريف Rural		Total		كلا الجنسين
	رجال Men	نساء Women	رجال Men	نساء Women	رجال Men	نساء Women	رجال Men	نساء Women	رجال Men	نساء Women	Both sexes
0-4	1 096 513	1 059 504	203 316	194 892	...	...	...	...	1 299 829	1 254 396	2 554 225
5-9	1 061 429	1 046 203	182 545	179 478	...	...	...	...	1 243 974	1 225 681	2 469 655
10-14	913 956	883 052	129 577	125 665	...	...	...	...	1 043 533	1 008 717	2 052 250
15-19	660 372	674 584	80 154	80 695	...	...	...	...	740 526	755 279	1 495 805
20-24	525 534	516 615	259 179	101 744	...	...	...	...	784 713	618 359	1 403 072
25-29	415 443	455 358	612 593	156 401	...	...	...	...	1 028 036	611 759	1 639 735
30-34	326 933	320 143	633 639	226 364	...	...	...	...	960 572	546 507	1 507 079
35-39	264 540	283 492	499 700	143 272	...	...	...	...	764 240	426 764	1 191 004
40-44	180 207	186 672	320 615	72 340	...	...	...	...	500 822	259 012	759 834
45-49	153 968	161 226	171 716	36 619	...	...	...	...	325 684	197 845	523 529
50-54	143 948	147 998	92 104	23 011	...	...	...	...	236 052	171 009	407 061
55-59	117 397	92 678	39 890	10 313	...	...	...	...	157 287	102 991	260 278
60-64	127 584	92 843	20 711	9 488	...	...	...	...	148 295	102 331	250 626
65-69	71 059	48 789	7 939	4 280	...	...	...	...	78 998	53 069	132 067
70-74	65 096	52 577	5 200	4 534	...	...	...	...	70 296	57 111	127 407
75+	91 814	72 526	5 302	5 059	...	...	...	...	97 116	77 585	174 701
غير محدد not stated	-	-	-	-	...	...	...	...	-	-	-
المجموع Total	6 215 793	6 094 260	3 264 180	1 374 155	...	...	...	...	9 479 973	7 468 415	16 948 388

-28-

2004 تعداد ،المملكة العربية السعودية بحسب الفئات العمرية في السكان
Table 25: Population of Saudi Arabia by age groups, 2004 census
جدول 25: السكان في المملكة العربية السعودية بحسب الفئات العمرية، تعداد 2004

Age group القئة العمرية	Nationals المواطنين		Non-nationals غير مواطنين		Urban حضر		Rural ريف		Total		
	Men رجال	Women نساء	Men رجال	Women نساء	Men رجال	Women نساء	Men رجال	Women نساء	Men رجال	Women نساء	Both sexes كلا الجنسين
0-4	1 066 010	1 054 525	223 381	215 747	...	...	...	...	1 289 391	1 270 272	2 559 663
5-9	1 127 253	1 112 582	207 007	197 901	...	...	...	...	1 334 260	1 310 483	2 644 743
10-14	1 081 884	1 155 728	176 568	167 659	...	...	...	...	1 258 452	1 323 387	2 581 839
15-19	948 707	938 982	150 298	142 200	...	...	...	...	1 099 005	1 081 182	2 180 187
20-24	760 146	786 510	298 251	159 920	...	...	...	...	1 058 397	946 430	2 004 827
25-29	725 413	701 326	626 706	240 156	...	...	...	...	1 352 119	941 482	2 293 601
30-34	569 152	575 126	709 730	271 093	...	...	...	...	1 278 882	846 219	2 125 101
35-39	492 543	498 170	674 734	190 103	...	...	...	...	1 167 277	688 273	1 855 550
40-44	411 890	372 981	511 983	121 907	...	...	...	...	923 873	494 888	1 418 761
45-49	313 340	277 511	338 148	72 775	...	...	...	...	651 488	350 286	1 001 774
50-54	222 166	199 415	193 133	43 516	...	...	...	...	415 299	242 931	658 230
55-59	146 079	153 194	84 880	21 644	...	...	...	...	230 959	174 838	405 797
60-64	126 594	134 390	39 555	14 973	...	...	...	...	166 149	149 363	315 512
65-69	103 245	101 213	16 678	7 846	...	...	...	...	119 923	109 059	228 982
70-74	77 277	84 898	9 837	6 381	...	...	...	...	87 114	91 279	178 393
75+	115 671	93 419	8 981	7 231	...	...	...	...	124 652	100 650	225 302
not stated غير محدد	-	-	-	-	...	...	...	...	-	-	-
Total المجموع	8 287 370	8 239 970	4 269 870	1 881 052	...	...	...	...	12 557 240	10 121 022	22 678 262

جدول 26: السكان في السودان حسب الفئات العمرية، تعداد 1993
Table 26: Population of Sudan by age groups, 1993 census

القئة العمرية Age group	المواطنين Nationals نساء Women	رجال Men	غير مواطنين Non-nationals نساء Women	رجال Men	حضر Urban نساء Women	رجال Men	ريف Rural نساء Women	رجال Men	المجموع Total نساء Women	رجال Men	كلا الجنسين Both sexes
0-4	...	...	...	...	439 215	454 369	1 148 692	1 169 733	1 587 907	1 624 102	3 212 009
5-9	...	...	...	...	456 925	467 702	1 229 339	1 296 421	1 686 264	1 764 123	3 450 387
10-14	...	...	...	...	404 336	427 856	962 681	1 079 671	1 367 017	1 507 527	2 874 544
15-19	...	...	...	...	382 512	411 410	752 599	754 105	1 135 111	1 165 515	2 300 626
20-24	...	...	...	...	338 926	385 865	593 414	466 392	932 340	852 257	1 784 597
25-29	...	...	...	...	311 201	310 804	606 510	405 617	917 711	716 421	1 634 132
30-34	...	...	...	...	196 196	257 706	397 917	332 792	594 113	590 498	1 184 611
35-39	...	...	...	...	198 560	223 250	426 488	344 459	625 048	567 709	1 192 757
40-44	...	...	...	...	121 294	145 782	288 168	257 873	409 462	403 655	813 117
45-49	...	...	...	...	114 400	128 957	249 621	227 184	364 021	356 141	720 162
50-54	...	...	...	...	85 205	98 743	201 631	204 580	286 836	303 323	590 159
55-59	...	...	...	...	50 706	62 582	107 179	125 486	157 885	188 068	345 953
60-64	...	...	...	...	50 241	60 257	125 094	143 798	175 335	204 055	379 390
65-69	...	...	...	...	30 974	38 522	70 066	97 007	101 040	135 529	236 569
70-74	...	...	...	...	29 500	30 959	79 096	90 845	108 596	121 804	230 400
75+	...	...	...	...	35 409	37 408	105 066	117 761	140 475	155 169	295 644
غير محدد not stated	...	...	...	...	1 879	4 612	3 985	11 107	5 864	15 719	21 583
المجموع Total	...	...	...	...	3 247 479	3 546 784	7 347 546	7 124 831	10 595 025	10 671 615	21 266 640

2008 جدول 27: السكان في السودان بحسب الفئات العمرية، تعداد
Table 27: Population of Sudan by age groups, 2008 census

القئة العمرية Age group	المواطنون / Nationals		غير مواطنين / Non-nationals		حضر / Urban		ريف / Rural		Total		كلا الجنسين Both sexes
	رجال Men	نساء Women	رجال Men	نساء Women	رجال Men	نساء Women	رجال Men	نساء Women	رجال Men	نساء Women	المجموع Both sexes
0-4	…	…	…	…	…	…	…	…	3 005 746	2 840 245	5 845 991
5-9	…	…	…	…	…	…	…	…	3 023 603	2 778 173	5 801 776
10-14	…	…	…	…	…	…	…	…	2 689 626	2 346 411	5 036 037
15-19	…	…	…	…	…	…	…	…	2 151 401	2 024 954	4 176 355
20-24	…	…	…	…	…	…	…	…	1 740 076	1 796 936	3 537 012
25-29	…	…	…	…	…	…	…	…	1 466 418	1 648 548	3 114 966
30-34	…	…	…	…	…	…	…	…	1 207 987	1 295 976	2 503 963
35-39	…	…	…	…	…	…	…	…	1 134 069	1 180 296	2 314 365
40-44	…	…	…	…	…	…	…	…	905 533	868 298	1 773 831
45-49	…	…	…	…	…	…	…	…	689 233	614 447	1 303 680
50-54	…	…	…	…	…	…	…	…	581 191	513 515	1 094 706
55-59	…	…	…	…	…	…	…	…	350 041	285 760	635 801
60-64	…	…	…	…	…	…	…	…	380 847	310 256	691 103
65-69	…	…	…	…	…	…	…	…	227 674	168 614	396 288
70-74	…	…	…	…	…	…	…	…	229 753	185 942	415 695
75+	…	…	…	…	…	…	…	…	290 779	222 142	512 921
غير محدد not stated	…	…	…	…	…	…	…	…	0	0	0
المجموع Total	…	…	…	…	…	…	…	…	20 073 977	19 080 513	39 154 490

-31-

جدول 28: السكان في الجمهورية العربية السورية بحسب الفئات العمرية، تعداد 1994
Table 28: Population of Syrian Arab Republic by age groups, 1994 census

القئة العمرية Age group	المواطنين Nationals رجال Men	نساء Women	غير مواطنين Non-nationals رجال Men	نساء Women	حضر Urban رجال Men	نساء Women	ريف Rural رجال Men	نساء Women	المجموع Total رجال Men	نساء Women	كلا الجنسين Both sexes
0-4	...	...	...	...	...	...	...	...	1 056 000	994 000	2 050 000
5-9	...	...	...	...	...	...	...	...	1 087 000	1 033 000	2 120 000
10-14	...	...	...	...	...	...	...	...	1 030 000	975 000	2 005 000
15-19	...	...	...	...	...	...	...	...	814 000	785 000	1 599 000
20-24	...	...	...	...	...	...	...	...	632 000	622 000	1 254 000
25-29	...	...	...	...	...	...	...	...	527 000	518 000	1 045 000
30-34	...	...	...	...	...	...	...	...	427 000	420 000	847 000
35-39	...	...	...	...	...	...	...	...	332 000	320 000	652 000
40-44	...	...	...	...	...	...	...	...	271 000	256 000	527 000
45-49	...	...	...	...	...	...	...	...	202 000	190 000	392 000
50-54	...	...	...	...	...	...	...	...	170 000	171 000	341 000
55-59	...	...	...	...	...	...	...	...	135 000	129 000	264 000
60-64	...	...	...	...	...	...	...	...	144 000	133 000	277 000
65+	...	...	...	...	...	...	...	...	222 000	187 000	409 000
غير محدد not stated	...	...	...	...	...	...	...	...	-	-	-
المجموع Total	...	...	...	...	...	...	...	...	7 049 000	6 733 000	13 782 000

2004 جدول 29: السكان في الجمهورية العربية السورية بحسب الفئات العمرية تعداد
Table 29: Population of Syrian Arab Republic by age groups, 2004 census

القئة العمرية Age group	المواطنون Nationals رجال Men	نساء Women	غير مواطنين Non-nationals رجال Men	نساء Women	حضر Urban رجال Men	نساء Women	ريف Rural رجال Men	نساء Women	المجموع Total رجال Men	المجموع نساء Women	كلا الجنسين Both sexes
0-4	...	...	...	...	644 000	609 000	629 000	594 000	1 273 000	1 203 000	2 476 000
5-9	...	...	...	...	633 000	596 000	602 000	568 000	1 235 000	1 164 000	2 399 000
10-14	...	...	...	...	578 000	539 000	536 000	501 000	1 114 000	1 040 000	2 154 000
15-19	...	...	...	...	560 000	532 000	518 000	491 000	1 078 000	1 023 000	2 101 000
20-24	...	...	...	...	504 000	486 000	444 000	430 000	948 000	916 000	1 864 000
25-29	...	...	...	...	393 000	380 000	334 000	329 000	727 000	709 000	1 436 000
30-34	...	...	...	...	335 000	325 000	262 000	258 000	597 000	583 000	1 180 000
35-39	...	...	...	...	296 000	284 000	220 000	216 000	516 000	500 000	1 016 000
40-44	...	...	...	...	259 000	239 000	168 000	169 000	427 000	408 000	835 000
45-49	...	...	...	...	198 000	178 000	129 000	129 000	327 000	307 000	634 000
50-54	...	...	...	...	159 000	137 000	109 000	112 000	268 000	249 000	517 000
55-59	...	...	...	...	109 000	96 000	80 000	76 000	189 000	172 000	361 000
60-64	...	...	...	...	85 000	78 000	65 000	68 000	150 000	146 000	296 000
65-69	...	...	...	...	62 000	54 000	49 000	47 000	111 000	101 000	212 000
70-74	...	...	...	...	52 000	46 000	50 000	46 000	102 000	92 000	194 000
75+	...	...	...	...	46 000	41 000	55 000	39 000	101 000	80 000	181000
غير محدد not stated	...	...	...	...	28 000	26 000	4 000	4 000	32 000	30 000	62 000
المجموع Total	...	...	...	...	4 941 000	4 646 000	4254 000	4077 000	9 195 000	8 723 000	17 918 000

1985 جدول السكان في الإمارات العربية المتحدة بحسب الفئات العمرية، تعداد
Table 30: Population of United Arab Emirates by age groups, 1985 census

القئة العمرية Age group	المواطنين Nationals رجال Men	نساء Women	غير مواطنين Non-nationals رجال Men	نساء Women	حضر Urban رجال Men	نساء Women	ريف Rural رجال Men	نساء Women	المجموع Total رجال Men	نساء Women	كلا الجنسين Both sexes
0-4	40 598	38 975	56 083	53 489	73 691	70 623	22 990	21 841	96 681	92 464	189 145
5-9	37 610	36 286	42 058	38 896	60 623	57 318	19 045	17 864	79 668	75 182	154 850
10-14	26 722	25 205	23 717	21 036	39 244	35 988	11 195	10 253	50 439	46 241	96 680
15-19	20 886	19 291	17 876	15 223	30 399	27 043	8 363	7 471	38 762	34 514	73 276
20-24	15 181	14 865	60 486	32 460	60 171	38 683	15 496	8 642	75 667	47 325	122 992
25-29	11 351	13 366	133 197	44 812	114 506	48 538	30 042	9 640	144 548	58 178	202 726
30-34	8 235	9 402	132 966	35 257	114 759	38 080	26 442	6 579	141 201	44 659	185 860
35-39	8 399	8 599	103 535	22 861	92 128	26 608	19 806	4 852	111 934	31 460	143 394
40-44	6 488	6 298	59 958	10 759	53 902	14 159	12 544	2 898	66 446	17 057	83 503
45-49	7 090	5 907	35 889	5 961	34 714	9 665	8 265	2 203	42 979	11 868	54 847
50-54	5 549	4 468	16 402	3343	17 525	6 021	4 426	1 790	21 951	7 811	29 762
55-59	3 911	3 000	6 646	1 952	8 379	3 854	2 178	1 098	10 557	4 952	15 509
60-64	3 128	2 616	2 414	1 467	4 187	3 003	1 355	1 080	5 542	4 083	9 625
65-69	2 733	1 988	985	1 000	2 531	2 175	1 187	813	3 718	2 988	6 706
70-74	2 132	1 705	546	600	1 702	1 648	976	657	2 678	2 305	4 983
75+	2 131	1 981	458	544	1 637	1 772	952	753	2 589	2 525	5 114
غير محدد not stated	13	5	227	86	213	88	27	3	240	91	331
المجموع Total	202 157	193 957	693 443	289 746	710 311	385 266	185 289	98 437	895 600	483 703	1 379 303

جدول 31: السكان في الإمارات العربية المتحدة بحسب الفئات العمرية، تعداد 1995

Table 31: Population of United Arab Emirates by age groups, 1995 census

القئة العمرية Age group	المواطنون Nationals		غير مواطنين Non-nationals		حضر Urban		ريف Rural		المجموع Total		كلا الجنسين Both sexes
	رجال Men	نساء Women	رجال Men	نساء Women	رجال Men	نساء Women	رجال Men	نساء Women	رجال Men	نساء Women	
0-4	44 663	42 488	64 861	61 037	82 880	78 198	26 644	25 327	109 524	103 525	213 049
5-9	45 450	43 461	67 534	62 846	85 413	80 455	27 571	25 852	112 984	106 307	219 291
10-14	46 845	44 628	58 040	52 541	78 500	72 948	26 385	24 221	104 885	97 169	202 054
15-19	42 871	40 778	40 567	34 693	60 744	56 717	22 694	18 754	83 438	75 471	158 909
20-24	28 255	29 043	111 613	48 839	107 485	63 597	32 383	14 285	139 868	77 882	217 750
25-29	19 836	20 159	218 268	68 250	186 342	74 380	51 762	14 029	238 104	88 409	326 513
30-34	13 262	14 836	215 804	65 377	179 601	68 284	49 465	11 929	229 066	80 213	309 279
35-39	11 904	15 044	208 057	53 696	172 904	58 250	47 057	10 490	219 961	68 740	288 701
40-44	8 976	9 964	152 607	31 682	128 593	35 423	32 990	6 223	161 583	41 646	203 229
45-49	8 815	8 445	97 351	17 405	85 075	21 742	21 091	4 108	106 166	25 850	132 016
50-54	6 676	6 036	44 979	7 658	41 165	11 168	10 490	2 526	51 655	13 694	65 349
55-59	5 866	4 490	19 180	3 854	19 946	6 724	5 100	1 620	25 046	8 344	33 390
60-64	4 182	3 372	6 225	2 181	8 061	4 166	2 346	1 387	10 407	5 553	15 960
65-69	3 940	2 870	2 552	1 727	4 839	3 432	1 653	1 165	6 492	4 597	11 089
70-74	2 578	2 099	1 073	1 081	2 498	2 216	1 153	0 964	3 651	3 180	6 831
75+	2 930	2 549	913	1 074	2 386	2 451	1 457	1 172	3 843	3 623	7 466
غير محدد not stated	11	8	120	26	98	27	33	7	131	34	165
المجموع Total	297 060	290 270	1 309 744	513 967	1 246 530	0 640 178	360 274	164 059	1 606 804	804 237	2 411 041

2005 جدول 32: السكان في الإمارات العربية المتحدة بحسب الفئات العمرية، تعداد
Table 32: Population of United Arab Emirates by age groups, 2005 census

الفئة العمرية Age group	النطنيون Nationals		غير مواطنين Non-nationals		حضر Urban		ريف Rural		المجموع Total		
	رجال Men	نساء Women	رجال Men	نساء Women	رجال Men	نساء Women	رجال Men	نساء Women	رجال Men	نساء Women	كلا الجنسين Both sexes
0-4	55 120	52 310	90 497	84 217	115 800	108 369	29 801	28 169	145 617	136 527	282 144
5-9	52 371	49 704	87 567	79 754	111 645	102 170	28 284	27 283	139 938	129 458	269 396
10-14	53 985	50 382	76 777	67 887	101 461	90 889	29 317	27 390	130 762	118 269	249 031
15-19	55 575	52 536	65 823	58 304	91 065	82 127	30 323	28 711	121 398	110 840	232 238
20-24	50 673	52 764	221 350	108 756	222 387	126 692	49 649	34 838	272 023	161 520	433 543
25-29	39 396	41 121	444 220	137 028	410 228	148 462	73 429	29 675	483 616	178 149	661 765
30-34	25 846	26 497	464 072	123 994	417 909	130 590	71 970	19 892	489 918	150 491	640 409
35-39	20 189	21 554	366 565	92 265	329 059	98 409	57 703	15 435	386 754	113 819	500 573
40-44	14 633	16 366	248 093	62 190	220 959	67 833	41 759	10 710	262 726	78 556	341 282
45-49	12 433	13 857	162 043	37 458	145 298	43 434	29 161	7 877	174 476	51 315	225 791
50-54	10 246	9 947	97 081	21 592	89 983	26 536	17 356	5 003	107 327	31 539	138 866
55-59	7 893	6 341	43 410	9 467	42 788	13 022	8 515	2 782	51 303	15 808	67 111
60-64	6 176	4 549	12 632	3 971	15 510	6 647	3 310	1 880	18 808	8 520	27 328
65-69	5 335	3 283	3 840	2 001	6 623	3 892	2 549	1 393	9 175	5 284	14 459
70-74	3 657	2 699	1 746	1 319	3 659	2 762	1 732	1 251	5 403	4 018	9 421
75+	3 739	2 995	1 250	1 440	4 532	4 099	2 377	2 064	4 989	4 435	9 424
غير معدد not stated	650	673	1269	1054	...	...	...	...	1919	1727	3646
المجموع Total	417 917	407 578	2388 235	892 697	2 328 906	1 055 933	477 235	244 353	2 806 152	1 300 275	4 106 427

جدول السكان في اليمن بحسب الفئات العمرية، تعداد 1994
Table 33: Population of Yemen by age groups, 1994 census

الفئة العمرية Age group	Nationals المواطنون		غير مواطنين Non-nationals		Urban حضر		Rural ريف		Total		المجموع
	رجال Men	نساء Women	رجال Men	نساء Women	رجال Men	نساء Women	رجال Men	نساء Women	رجال Men	نساء Women	كلا الجنسين Both sexes
0-4	:	:	:	:	:	:	:	:	1 215 937	1 179 206	2 395 143
5-9	:	:	:	:	:	:	:	:	1 404 565	1 331 482	2 736 047
10-14	:	:	:	:	:	:	:	:	1 186 356	1 016 690	2 203 046
15-19	:	:	:	:	:	:	:	:	785 210	701 654	1 486 864
20-24	:	:	:	:	:	:	:	:	514 211	475 867	990 078
25-29	:	:	:	:	:	:	:	:	433 696	480 509	914 205
30-34	:	:	:	:	:	:	:	:	370 705	409 873	780 578
35-39	:	:	:	:	:	:	:	:	357 799	381 442	739 241
40-44	:	:	:	:	:	:	:	:	267 085	267 883	534 968
45-49	:	:	:	:	:	:	:	:	212 529	207 928	420 457
50-54	:	:	:	:	:	:	:	:	193 656	190 170	383 826
55-59	:	:	:	:	:	:	:	:	109 384	98 220	207 604
60-64	:	:	:	:	:	:	:	:	149 950	134 802	284 752
65-69	:	:	:	:	:	:	:	:	72 669	62 219	134 888
70-74	:	:	:	:	:	:	:	:	89 839	82 172	172 011
75+	:	:	:	:	:	:	:	:	109 949	100 150	210 099
غير محدد not stated	:	:	:	:	:	:	:	:	-	-	-
المجموع Total	...	...	...	...	...	...	...	...	7 473 540	7 120 267	14 593 807

-37-

جدول 34: السكان في اليمن بحسب الفئات العمرية، تعداد 2004
Table 34: Population of Yemen by age groups, 2004 census

القئة العمرية Age group	المواطنون Nationals رجال Men	نساء Women	غير مواطنين Non-nationals رجال Men	نساء Women	حضر Urban رجال Men	نساء Women	ريف Rural رجال Men	نساء Women	المجموع Total رجال Men	المجموع Women	المجموع Both sexes كلا الجنسين
0-4	1 495 907	1 431 580	5 391	5 269	:	:	:	:	1 501 298	1 436 849	2 938 147
5-9	1 563 176	1 483 616	3 996	3 776	:	:	:	:	1 567 172	1 487 392	3 054 564
10-14	1 509 907	1 351 926	3 571	3 359	:	:	:	:	1 513 478	1 355 285	2 868 763
15-19	1 260 787	1 207 570	4 126	3 667	:	:	:	:	1 264 913	1 211 237	2 476 150
20-24	960 318	920 894	5 681	4 768	:	:	:	:	965 999	925 662	1 891 661
25-29	725 065	736 659	4 571	4 778	:	:	:	:	729 636	741 437	1 471 073
30-34	483 419	475 573	4 078	3 907	:	:	:	:	487 497	479 480	966 977
35-39	426 646	473 942	3 875	3 318	:	:	:	:	430 521	477 260	907 781
40-44	351 163	370 483	3 607	2 558	:	:	:	:	354 770	373 041	727 811
45-49	280 817	299 556	2 794	1 543	:	:	:	:	283 611	301 099	584 710
50-54	252 682	242 859	2 055	1 231	:	:	:	:	254 737	244 090	498 827
55-59	148 959	136 710	1 147	650	:	:	:	:	150 106	137 360	287 466
60-64	169 675	153 587	731	626	:	:	:	:	170 406	154 213	324 619
65-69	96 225	86 221	335	300	:	:	:	:	96 560	86 521	183 081
70-74	113 862	104 159	279	319	:	:	:	:	114 141	104 478	218 619
75+	144 496	127 498	278	387	:	:	:	:	144 774	127 885	272 659
غير محدد not stated	6 677	4 676	657	243	:	:	:	:	7 334	4 919	12 253
المجموع Total	9 989 781	9 607 509	47 172	40 699	...	...	...	...	10 036 953	9 648 208	19 685 161

جدول التعدادات السكانية (مواطنون، غير مواطنين) (حضر، ريف) البحرين :35

Table 35: Population censuses (nationals, non-nationals) (urban, rural): Bahrain

السنة Year	المواطنون Nationals		غير مواطنين Non-nationals		حضر Urban		ريف Rural		المجموع Total
	Men رجال	Women نساء	Men رجال	Women نساء	Men رجال	Women نساء	Men رجال	Women نساء	
1991	163 453	159 852	130 893	53 839	…	…	…	…	508 037
2001	204 623	201 044	169 026	75 911	…	…	…	…	650 604

جدول التعدادات السكانية (مواطنون، غير مواطنين) (حضر، ريف) مصر :36

Table 36: Population censuses (nationals, non-nationals) (urban, rural): Egypt

السنة Year	المواطنون Nationals		غير مواطنين Non-nationals		حضر Urban		ريف Rural		المجموع Total
	Men رجال	Women نساء	Men رجال	Women نساء	Men رجال	Women نساء	Men رجال	Women نساء	
1986	…	…	…	…	10 908 849	10 306 654	13 800 424	13 238 310	48 254 237
1996	…	…	…	…	12 957 775	12 328 560	17 393 615	16 632 964	59 312 914
2006	36 508 599	34 839 062	64 368	51 326	…	…	…	…	71 463 355

جدول التعدادات السكانية (مواطنون، غير مواطنين) (حضر، ريف) العراق :37

Table 37: Population censuses (nationals, non-nationals) (urban, rural): Iraq

السنة Year	المواطنون Nationals		غير مواطنين Non-nationals		حضر Urban		ريف Rural		المجموع Total
	Men رجال	Women نساء	Men رجال	Women نساء	Men رجال	Women نساء	Men رجال	Women نساء	
1987	…	…	…	…	5 951 403	5 517 566	2 444 486	2 421 744	16 335 199
1997	…	…	…	…	7 542 510	7 526 538	3 444 741	3 532 455	22 046 244

جدول ٣٨: التعدادات السكانية (مواطنون، غير مواطنين) (حضر، ريف) الأردن

Table 38: Population censuses (nationals, non-nationals) (urban, rural): Jordan

السنة Year	Nationals المواطنون		Non-nationals غير مواطنين		Urban حضر		Rural ريف		Total المجموع
	Men رجال	Women نساء	Men رجال	Women نساء	Men رجال	Women نساء	Men رجال	Women نساء	ع
1994	2 160 725	1 978 733	209 068	105 897	1 687 530	1 551 227	473 195	427 533	4 454 423
2004	2 394 947	2 316 419	231 340	160 933	2 055 431	1 941 952	570 856	535 400	5 103 639

جدول ٣٩: التعدادات السكانية (مواطنون، غير مواطنين) (حضر، ريف) الكويت

Table 39: Population censuses (nationals, non-nationals) (urban, rural): Kuwait

السنة Year	Nationals المواطنون		Non-nationals غير مواطنين		Urban حضر		Rural ريف		Total المجموع
	Men رجال	Women نساء	Men رجال	Women نساء	Men رجال	Women نساء	Men رجال	Women نساء	ع
1985	241 919	232 292	727 026	496 712	…	…	…	…	1 697 949
1995	1 197 429	1 144 497	587 101	334 853	…	…	…	…	3 263 880
2005	425 225	435 045	875 068	458 259	…	…	…	…	2 193 597

جدول ٤٠: التعدادات السكانية (مواطنون، غير مواطنين) (حضر، ريف) عمان

Table 40: Population censuses (nationals, non-nationals) (urban, rural): Oman

السنة Year	Nationals المواطنون		Non-nationals غير مواطنين		Urban حضر		Rural ريف		Total المجموع
	Men رجال	Women نساء	Men رجال	Women نساء	Men رجال	Women نساء	Men رجال	Women نساء	ع
1993	755 110	728 116	422 895	111 953	860 985	585 373	317 020	254 696	2 013 074
2003	900 540	881 018	412 699	146 558	950 471	723 009	362 768	304 567	2 343 815

جدول التعدادات السكانية (مواطنين، غير مواطنين) (حضر، ريف): فلسطين :41

Table 41: Population censuses (nationals, non-nationals) (urban, rural): Palestine

السنة Year	Nationals		Non-nationals		Urban		Rural		المجموع Total
	المواطنين	غير مواطنين		حضر		ريف		
	Men رجال	Women نساء	Men رجال	Women نساء	Men رجال	Women نساء	Men رجال	Women نساء	
1997	1320 988	1276 628	1 276	2 777					2 601 669
2007	...	...	...	...	...	...	...	...	3 767 125

جدول التعدادات السكانية (مواطنين، غير مواطنين) (حضر، ريف): قطر :42

Table 42: Population censuses (nationals, non-nationals) (urban, rural): Qatar

السنة Year	Nationals		Non-nationals		Urban		Rural		المجموع Total
	المواطنين	غير مواطنين		حضر		ريف		
	Men رجال	Women نساء	Men رجال	Women نساء	Men رجال	Women نساء	Men رجال	Women نساء	
1986	...	...	...	...	...	...	...	...	369 079
2004	...	...	...	...	...	...	...	...	744 029

جدول التعدادات السكانية (مواطنين، غير مواطنين) (حضر، ريف): المملكة العربية السعودية :43

Table 43: Population censuses (nationals, non-nationals) (urban, rural): Saudi Arabia

السنة Year	Nationals		Non-nationals		Urban		Rural		المجموع Total
	المواطنين	غير مواطنين		حضر		ريف		
	Men رجال	Women نساء	Men رجال	Women نساء	Men رجال	Women نساء	Men رجال	Women نساء	
1992	6 215 793	6 094 260	3 264 180	1 374 155			...	...	16 948 388
2004	8 287 370	8 239 970	4 269 870	1 881 052			...	...	22 678 262

جدول 44: التعدادات السكانية (مواطنون، غير مواطنين) (حضر، ريف): السودان

Table 44: Population censuses (nationals, non-nationals) (urban, rural): Sudan

Year	Nationals Men	Nationals Women	Non-nationals Men	Non-nationals Women	Urban Men	Urban Women	Rural Men	Rural Women	Total
1993	...	...	...	...	...	...	...	...	21 266 340
2008	...	...	...	...	3546 784	3247 479	7124 831	7347 546	39 154 490

جدول 45: التعدادات السكانية (مواطنون، غير مواطنين) (حضر، ريف): الجمهورية العربية السورية

Table 45: Population censuses (nationals, non-nationals) (urban, rural): Syrian Arab Republic

Year	Nationals Men	Nationals Women	Non-nationals Men	Non-nationals Women	Urban Men	Urban Women	Rural Men	Rural Women	Total
1994	...	...	...	...	...	...	...	...	13 782 000
2004	...	...	...	...	4 941 000	4 646 000	4 254 000	4 077 000	17 916 000

جدول 46: التعدادات السكانية (مواطنون، غير مواطنين) (حضر، ريف): الإمارات العربية المتحدة

Table 46: Population censuses (nationals, non-nationals) (urban, rural): United Arab Emirates

Year	Nationals Men	Nationals Women	Non-nationals Men	Non-nationals Women	Urban Men	Urban Women	Rural Men	Rural Women	Total
1985	202 157	193 957	693 443	289 746	710 311	385 266	185 289	483 703	1 379 303
1995	297 060	290 270	1309 744	513 967	1 246 530	640 178	360 274	164 059	2 411 041
2005	417 917	407 578	2388 235	892 697	2 328 906	1 055 933	477 235	244 353	4 106 427

جدول 47: التعدادات السكانية (مواطنون، غير مواطنون) (حضر، ريف): اليمن

Table 47: Population censuses (nationals, non-nationals) (urban, rural): Yemen

السنة Year	Nationals المواطنون		Non-nationals غير مواطنين		Urban حضر		Rural ريف		المجموع ع Total
	Men رجال	Women نساء	Men رجال	Women نساء	Men رجال	Women نساء	Men رجال	Women نساء	
1994	...	...	...	...	...	...	...	...	14 593 807
2004	9 989 781	9 607 509	47 172	40 699	...	...	...	...	19 685 161

جدول 48: النسبة المئوية للشباب (في الفئة العمرية 24-15) لمجموع السكان خلال سنوات التعداد

Table 48: Percentage of youth population (in the age group 15-24) to total population during the census years

Country	1st census			2nd census			3rd census		
	census year سنة التعداد	% men youth نسبة الرجال الشباب	% women youth نسبة النساء الشباب	census year سنة التعداد	% men youth نسبة الرجال الشباب	% women youth نسبة النساء الشباب	census year سنة التعداد	% men youth نسبة الرجال الشباب	% women youth نسبة النساء الشباب
Bahrain البحرين	1991	8.57	7.65	2001	8.99	7.87	...	...	...
Egypt مصر	1986	10.19	9.11	1996	10.53	9.66	2006	10.54	9.64
Iraq العراق	1987	11.04	9.92	1997	10.49	10.32	...	...	...
Jordan الأردن	1994	12.29	10.45	2004	11.12	10.44	...	...	...
Kuwait الكويت	1985	8.85	8.48	1995	3.84	3.63	2005	8.86	7.38
Oman عمان	1993	8.94	7.45	2003	11.43	10.77	...	...	...
Palestine فلسطين	1997	10.11	9.49	2007	10.32	9.87	...	...	...
Qatar قطر	1986	9.34	5.62	2004	8.34	5.33	...	...	...
Saudi Arabia المملكة العربية السعودية	1992	9.00	8.10	2004	9.51	8.94	...	...	...
Sudan السودان	1993	9.49	9.72	2008	9.94	9.76	...	...	...
Syrian Arab Republic الجمهورية العربية السورية	1994	10.49	10.21	2004	11.31	10.82	...	...	...
United Arab Emirates الإمارات العربية المتحدة	1985	8.30	5.93	1995	9.26	6.36	2005	9.58	6.63
Yemen اليمن	1994	8.90	8.07	2004	11.33	10.86	...	...	...

جدول 49: النسبة المئوية للشباب (في الفئة العمرية 15-24) للسكان العاملين (في الفئة العمرية 15-64) خلال سنوات التعداد

Table 49: Percentage of youth population (in the age group 15-24) to woking population (in the age group 15-64) during the census years

Country	البلد	1st census التعداد الأول			2nd census التعداد الثاني			3rd census التعداد الثالث		
		census year سنة التعداد	% men نسبة الرجال	% women نسبة النساء	census year سنة التعداد	% men نسبة الرجال	% women نسبة النساء	census year سنة التعداد	% men نسبة الرجال	% women نسبة النساء
Bahrain	البحرين	1991	12.96	11.57	2001	12.91	11.30	…	…	…
Egypt	مصر	1986	18.14	16.22	1996	17.87	16.40	2006	17.89	16.36
Iraq	العراق	1987	22.04	19.81	1997	20.28	19.96	…	…	…
Jordan	الأردن	1994	21.47	18.26	2004	18.71	17.57	…	…	…
Kuwait	الكويت	1985	14.25	13.65	1995	11.61	10.97	2005	12.07	10.05
Oman	عمان	1993	15.77	13.13	2003	17.99	16.94	…	…	…
Palestine	فلسطين	1997	20.44	19.19	2007	19.80	18.94	…	…	…
Qatar	قطر	1986	13.11	7.89	2004	10.94	6.99	…	…	…
Saudi Arabia	المملكة العربية السعودية	1992	16.16	14.55	2004	15.13	14.22	…	…	…
Sudan	السودان	1993	18.43	18.89	2008	18.40	18.07	…	…	…
Syrian Arab Republic	الجمهورية العربية السورية	1994	20.09	19.55	2004	19.79	18.94	…	…	…
United Arab Emirates	الإمارات العربية المتحدة	1985	12.42	8.88	1995	12.75	8.76	2005	12.04	8.33
Yemen	اليمن	1994	19.27	17.46	2004	22.01	21.08	…	…	…

جدول 50: النسبة المئوية للمسنين (في الفئة العمرية +65) لمجموع السكان خلال سنوات التعداد

Table 50: Percentage of elderly population (in the age group 65+) to total population during the census years

Country	1st census census year	% men	% women	2nd census census year	% men	% women	3rd census census year	% men	% women	البلد
Bahrain	1991	1.20	1.04	2001	1.27	1.24	...	...	...	البحرين
Egypt	1986	1.74	1.57	1996	1.79	1.60	2006	1.79	1.60	مصر
Iraq	1987	1.65	1.82	1997	1.50	1.90	...	...	...	العراق
Jordan	1994	1.21	1.21	2004	1.63	1.60	...	...	...	الأردن
Kuwait	1985	0.63	0.42	1995	27.08	25.40	2005	0.89	0.78	الكويت
Oman	1993	1.14	1.12	2003	1.37	1.21	...	...	...	عمان
Palestine	1997	1.54	1.93	2007	1.27	1.70	...	...	...	فلسطين
Qatar	1986	0.59	0.43	2004	0.76	0.45	...	...	...	قطر
Saudi Arabia	1992	1.45	1.11	2004	1.46	1.33	...	...	...	المملكة العربية السعودية
Sudan	1993	1.94	1.65	2008	1.91	1.47	...	...	...	السودان
Syrian Arab Republic	1994	1.61	1.36	2004	1.75	1.52	...	...	...	الجمهورية العربية السورية
United Arab Emirates	1985	0.65	0.57	1995	0.58	0.47	2005	0.48	0.33	الإمارات العربية المتحدة
Yemen	1994	1.87	1.68	2004	1.81	1.62	...	...	...	اليمن

جدول 51: النسبة المئوية للإعالة لمجموع السكان خلال سنوات التعداد

Table 51: Percentage of dependency to total population during the census years

Country	1st census			2nd census			3rd census			البلد
	census year سنة التعداد	% men dependent نسبة الإعالة لدى الرجال	% women dependent نسبة الإعالة لدى النساء	census year سنة التعداد	% men dependent نسبة الإعالة لدى الرجال	% women dependent نسبة الإعالة لدى النساء	census year سنة التعداد	% men dependent نسبة الإعالة لدى الرجال	% women dependent نسبة الإعالة لدى النساء	
Bahrain	1991	26.41	24.89	2001	22.31	21.35	...	...	...	البحرين
Egypt	1986	39.83	37.21	1996	36.02	33.67	2006	36.05	33.68	مصر
Iraq	1987	49.48	47.68	1997	47.01	46.35	...	...	...	العراق
Jordan	1994	38.14	36.40	2004	34.93	33.30	...	...	...	الأردن
Kuwait	1985	31.17	29.77	1995	104.26	98.12	2005	18.82	17.45	الكويت
Oman	1993	38.81	37.48	2003	29.32	27.99	...	...	...	عمان
Palestine	1997	51.84	50.22	2007	44.94	44.04	...	...	...	فلسطين
Qatar	1986	20.85	19.57	2004	16.01	15.13	...	...	...	قطر
Saudi Arabia	1992	40.62	38.95	2004	29.55	29.49	...	...	...	المملكة العربية السعودية
Sudan	1993	48.50	45.60	2008	44.77	40.39	...	...	...	السودان
Syrian Arab Republic	1994	47.17	44.30	2004	38.44	35.94	...	...	...	الجمهورية العربية السورية
United Arab Emirates	1985	25.59	24.06	1995	19.50	18.18	2005	13.33	12.18	الإمارات العربية المتحدة
Yemen	1994	60.50	55.94	2004	48.71	45.36	...	...	...	اليمن

الهرم السكاني لبلدان الإسكوا
Population Pyramid in ESCWA countries

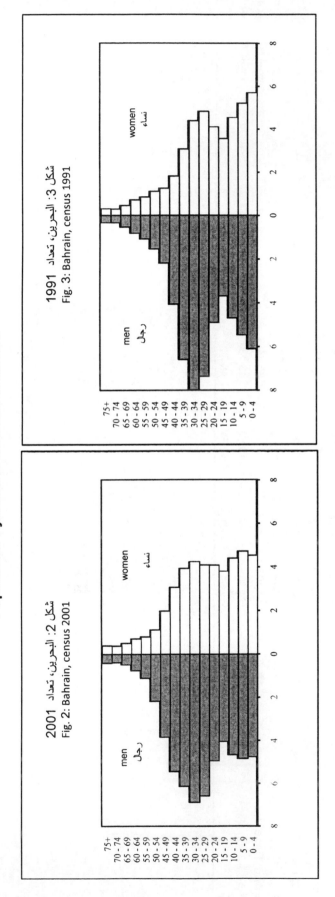

2001 البحرين، تعداد :2 شكل
Fig. 2: Bahrain, census 2001

1991 البحرين، تعداد :3 شكل
Fig. 3: Bahrain, census 1991

الهرم السكاني لبلدان الإسكوا (تابع)

Population Pyramid in ESCWA countries (cont'd)

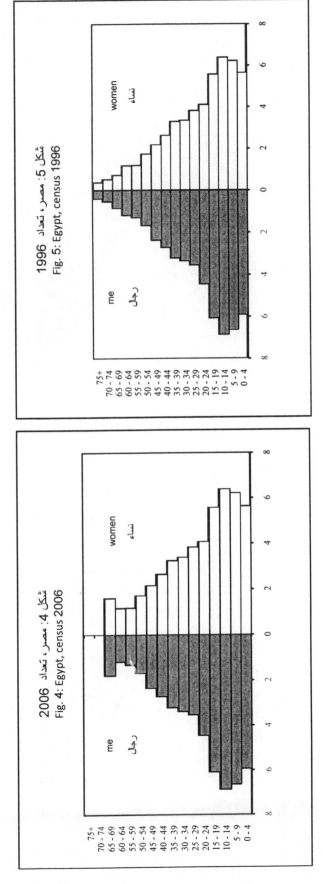

شكل 4: مصر، تعداد 2006
Fig. 4: Egypt, census 2006

شكل 5: مصر، تعداد 1996
Fig. 5: Egypt, census 1996

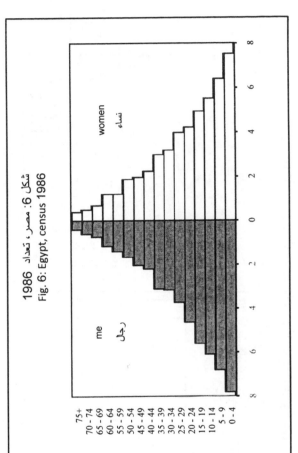

شكل 6: مصر، تعداد 1986
Fig. 6: Egypt, census 1986

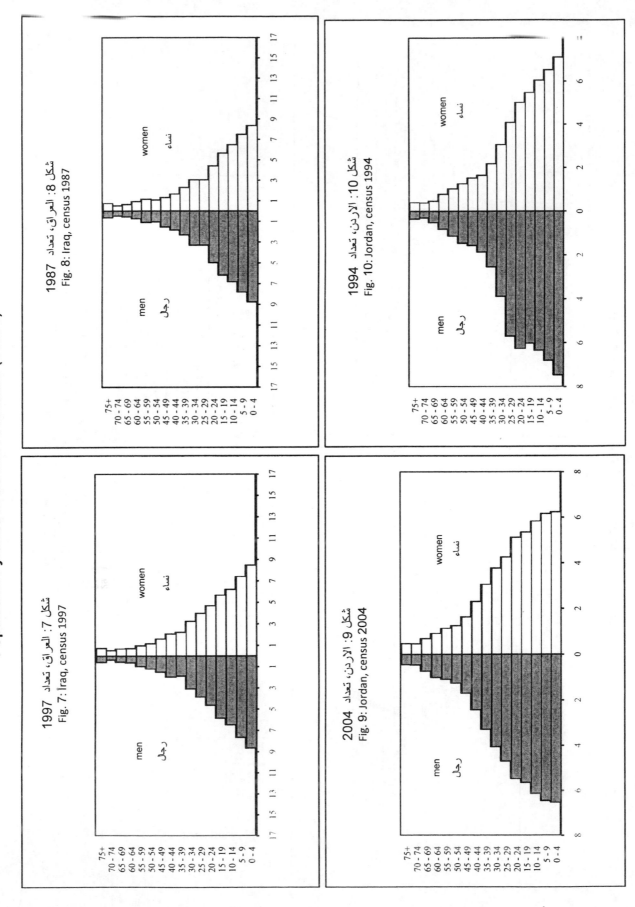

الهرم السكاني لبلدان الإسكوا (تابع)

Population Pyramid in ESCWA countries (cont'd)

1987 العراق، تعداد

Fig. 8: Iraq, census 1987

شكل :8 العراق

women نساء

men رجال

1994 الأردن، تعداد

Fig. 10: Jordan, census 1994

شكل :10 الأردن

women نساء

men رجال

1997 العراق، تعداد

Fig. 7: Iraq, census 1997

شكل :7 العراق

women نساء

men رجال

2004 الأردن، تعداد

Fig. 9: Jordan, census 2004

شكل :9 الأردن

women نساء

men رجال

الهرم السكاني لبلدان الإسكوا (تابع)
Population Pyramid in ESCWA countries (cont'd)

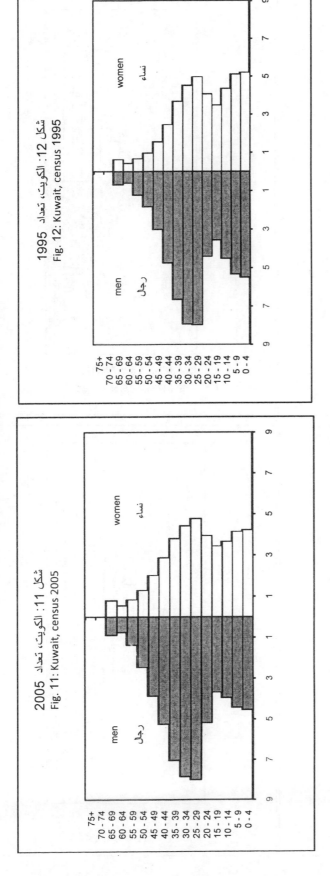

شكل الكويت :11 تعداد 2005
Fig. 11: Kuwait, census 2005

شكل الكويت :12 تعداد 1995
Fig. 12: Kuwait, census 1995

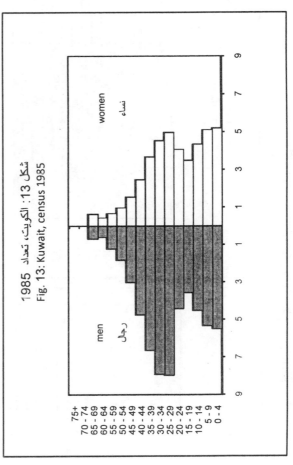

شكل الكويت :13 تعداد 1985
Fig. 13: Kuwait, census 1985

الهرم السكاني لبلدان الإسكوا (تابع)

Population Pyramid in ESCWA countries (cont'd)

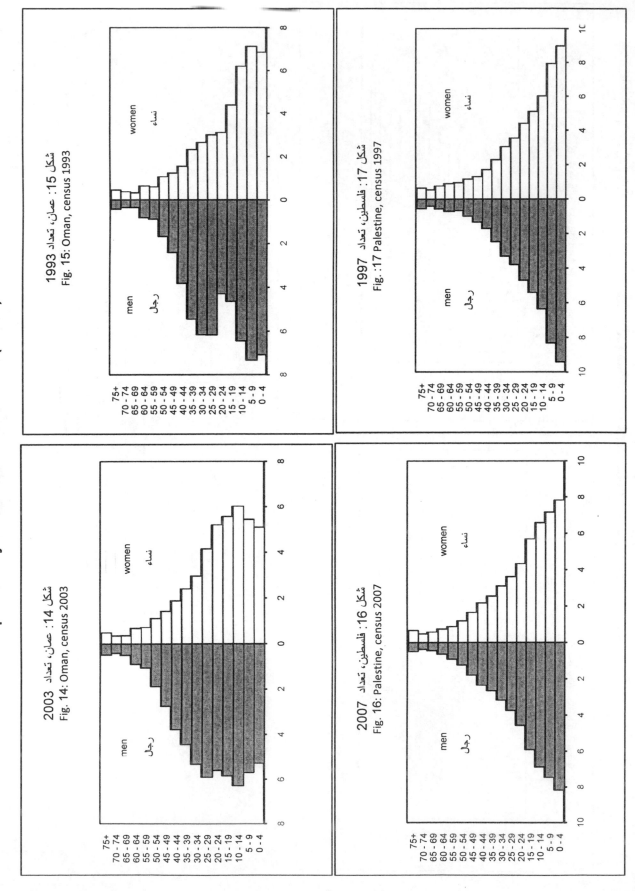

شكل 14: عمان تعداد 2003
Fig. 14: Oman, census 2003

شكل 15: عمان تعداد 1993
Fig. 15: Oman, census 1993

شكل 16: فلسطين، تعداد 2007
Fig. 16: Palestine, census 2007

شكل 17: فلسطين، تعداد 1997
Fig. :17 Palestine, census 1997

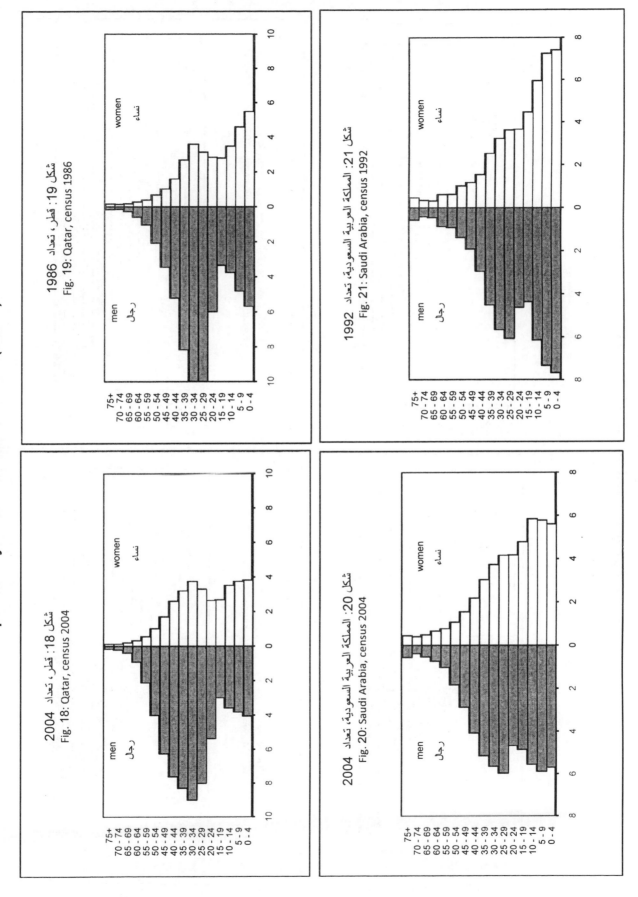

الهرم السكاني لبلدان الإسكوا (تابع)

Population Pyramid in ESCWA countries (cont'd)

شكل 18: قطر، تعداد 2004
Fig. 18: Qatar, census 2004

1986 قطر، تعداد 19: شكل
Fig. 19: Qatar, census 1986

شكل 20: المملكة العربية السعودية تعداد 2004
Fig. 20: Saudi Arabia, census 2004

1992 المملكة العربية السعودية تعداد 21: شكل
Fig. 21: Saudi Arabia, census 1992

الهرم السكاني لبلدان الإسكوا (تابع)

Population Pyramid in ESCWA countries (cont'd)

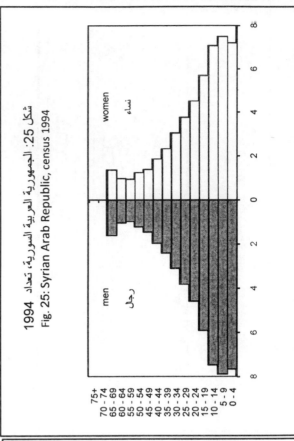

شكل 23: السودان، تعداد 1993
Fig.23: Sudan, census 1993

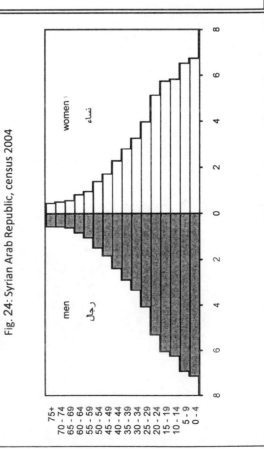

شكل 25: الجمهورية العربية السورية، تعداد 1994
Fig. 25: Syrian Arab Republic, census 1994

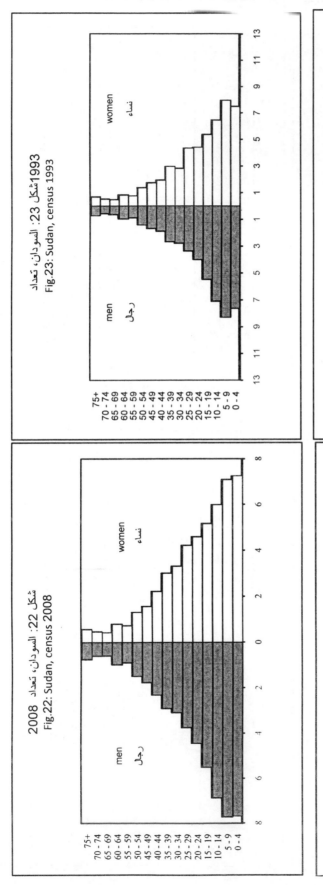

شكل 22: السودان، تعداد 2008
Fig.22: Sudan, census 2008

شكل 24: الجمهورية العربية السورية، تعداد 2004
Fig. 24: Syrian Arab Republic, census 2004

الهرم السكاني لبلدان الإسكوا (تابع)

Population Pyramid in ESCWA countries (cont'd)

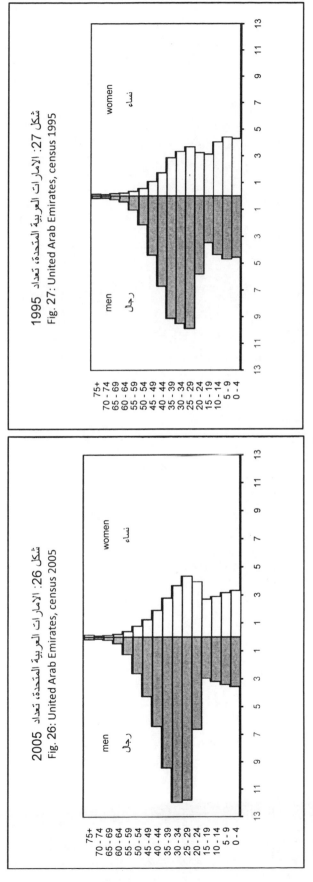

شكل 26: الإمارات العربية المتحدة تعداد 2005
Fig. 26: United Arab Emirates, census 2005

شكل 27: الإمارات العربية المتحدة تعداد 1995
Fig. 27: United Arab Emirates, census 1995

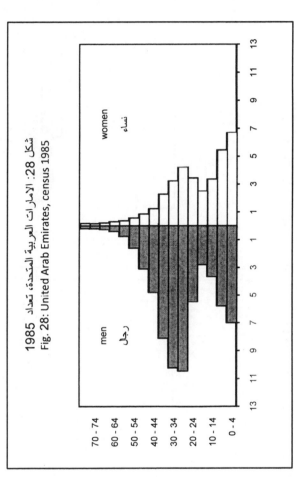

شكل 28: الإمارات العربية المتحدة تعداد 1985
Fig. 28: United Arab Emirates, census 1985

الهرم السكاني لبلدان الإسكوا (تابع) (تابع)

Population Pyramid in ESCWA countries (cont'd)

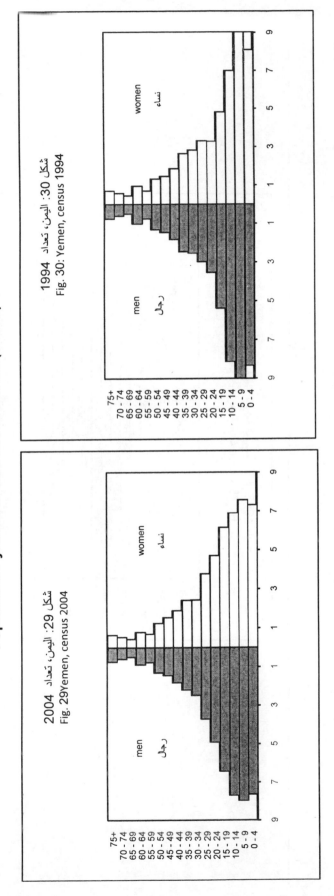

شكل 30: اليمن، تعداد 1994
Fig. 30: Yemen, census 1994

شكل 29: اليمن، تعداد 2004
Fig. 29Yemen, census 2004

القسم الثاني
Section Two

الخصوبة والوفيات
Fertility and Mortality

Section II is on Fertility and Mortality. It presents data on births and fertility, deaths and causes of death in the ESCWA region for the years 1990, 1995 and from 2000 to the most recent year, for available data in each country[1]. This section contains 30 tables and 23 graphs.

Data on registered number of live births, number of deaths, number of foetal, infant and child deaths, including the calculated crude birth rate (CBR), crude death rate (CDR), rate of natural increase (RNI), foetal and infant and child mortality rates for each member country have been presented.

In addition to this, the section presents data on general fertility rate (GFR), total fertility rate (TFR), adolescent fertility, gross reproduction rate (GRR), and mean age of childbearing for the years 1990, 1995, and from 2000 to the most recent year.

Finally,, distribution of causes of death by nationality and sex classified in accordance to the International Classification of Diseases (revision 10) have been presented.

يعرض القسم الثاني المعنون "الخصوبة والوفيات وأسباب الوفاة" بيانات عن المواليد الأحياء والخصوبة، والوفيات وأسباب الوفاة في منطقة الإسكوا للأعوام 1990 و1995 ومن عام 2000 وحتى آخر سنة تتوافر فيها البيانات عن كل بلد[1]. ويحتوي هذا القسم على 30 جدول و23 رسم بياني.

ثم عرض بيانات عن الولادات الحية والوفيات والمعدلات الخام للولادات، والمعدلات الخام للوفيات، ومعدلات وفيات الأجنة والرضّع، والأطفال لكل بلد من البلدان الأعضاء.

ويعرض هذا القسم أيضا بيانات عن المعدل العام للخصوبة ومعدل الخصوبة الإجمالي للإنجاب، ومتوسط عمر الإنجاب عند الحمل للأعوام 1995 و1990 ومنذ عام 2000 حتى آخر سنة متوفرة.

وكذلك ثم عرض بيانات عن الوفيات المسببة حسب الجنسية والجنس، وفقا للتصنيف الدولي للأمراض (المراجعة العاشرة).

-58-

(1) Only those countries for which relevant data are available have been included in the tables.

(1) أدرجت في الجداول فقط البلدان التي تتوافر بشأنها المعلومات.

جدول 52: المواليد الأحياء في بلدان الإسكوا 1990-2008

Table 52: Live Births in ESCWA Countries 1990-2008

	1990	1995	2000	2001	2002	2003	2004	2005	2006	2007	2008	
Bahrain	13 370	13 481	13 947	13 468	13 576	14 560	14 968	15 198	15 053	16 062	17 022	البحرين
Egypt	1 686 877	1 604 835	1 751 854	1 741 308	1 766 589	1 777 418	1 779 500	1 800 972	1 853 746	1 949 569	…	مصر
Iraq	660 385	455 727	471 886	716 861	746 771	691 269	840 257	896 340				العراق
Jordan	110 697	141 319	126 016	142 956	146 077	148 294	150 248	152 276	162 972	185 011	181 328	الأردن
Kuwait	…	40 790	41 843	41 342	43 490	43 982	47 274	50 941	52 759	53 587	…	الكويت
Lebanon	70 903	91 196	87 795	83 693	76 405	71 702	73 900	73 973	72 790	80 896	84 823	لبنان
Oman	51 943	57 859	39 994	39 297	40 222	40 062	40 584	42 065	49 499	52 619	58 250	عمان
Palestine	83 165	104 470	104 646	103 780	106 511	106 355	111 245	109 439	108 874	113 097	…	فلسطين
Qatar	11 022	10 371	11 250	12 118	12 200	12 856	13 190	13 401	14 120	15 681	17 210	قطر
Saudi Arabia	364 686	552 778	547 637	554 147	560 746	567 433	574 211	582 582	589 223	595 099	598 126	المملكة العربية السعودية
Sudan						150 218	376 158	283 576				السودان
Syrian Arab Republic	414 667	478 308	505 484	524 212	574 918	609 774	598 221	634 170	656 599	727 439	…	الجمهورية العربية السورية
United Arab Emirates	52 264	48 567	53 686	56 136	58 070	61 165	63 113	64 623	62 969	67 689	…	الإمارات العربية المتحدة
Yemen	577 781	95 354	252 895	260 106	189 341	130 112	153 945	152 792	275 716			اليمن
TOTAL	4 097 760	3 695 055	4 008 933	4 289 424	4 334 916	4 425 200	4 836 814	4 872 348	3 914 320	3 856 749	956 759	المجموع

جدول 53: معدل المواليد الأحياء الخام لكل ألف من السكان في بلدان الإسكوا 1990-2008

Table 53: Crude Birth Rate (per '000) population in ESCWA Countries 1990-2008

	1990	1995	2000	2001	2002	2003	2004	2005	2006	2007	2008	
Bahrain	27.1	23.3	21.5	20.3	20.0	20.9	21.0	20.9	20.2	21.1	21.9	البحرين
Egypt	29.2	25.1	25.0	24.3	24.2	23.9	23.5	23.3	23.6	24.4	…	مصر
Iraq	36.5	21.7	19.1	28.2	28.6	25.7	30.5	31.7				العراق
Jordan	34.0	32.8	26.0	28.7	28.6	28.3	27.8	27.4	28.4	31.1	29.6	الأردن
Kuwait	…	23.6	18.8	17.7	17.8	18.1	18.1	18.9	19.0	18.8	…	الكويت
Lebanon	23.8	26.1	23.3	21.8	19.6	18.1	18.3	18.1	17.6	19.4	20.2	لبنان
Oman	28.2	26.6	16.6	16.1	16.2	15.9	15.8	16.1	18.5	19.3	20.9	عمان
Palestine	38.6	39.9	33.2	31.8	31.4	30.3	30.6	29.1	28.0	28.2	…	فلسطين
Qatar	23.6	19.7	18.2	18.7	17.8	17.6	16.5	15.1	14.1	13.8	13.4	قطر
Saudi Arabia	22.4	30.3	26.3	25.9	25.6	25.2	24.9	24.7	24.4	24.1	23.7	المملكة العربية السعودية
Sudan						4.0	9.9	7.3				السودان
Syrian Arab Republic	32.6	32.7	30.6	30.9	33.0	34.0	32.3	33.2	33.2	35.5	…	الجمهورية العربية السورية
United Arab Emirates	28.0	20.0	16.6	16.4	16.2	16.2	16.0	15.8	14.9	15.5	…	الإمارات العربية المتحدة
Yemen	46.9	6.1	13.9	13.9	9.8	6.6	7.5	7.3	12.7			اليمن

Calculations are made on the basis of population estimates taken from the
United Nations World Population Prospects: the 2008 Revision

حُسبت المعدلات استنادا إلى تقديرات السكان الواردة في منشور الأمم المتحدة "التوقعات السكانية في العالم: تنقيح عام 2008"

جدول 54: الوفيات في بلدان الإسكوا 1990-2008
Table 54: Deaths in ESCWA Countries 1990-2008

	1990	1995	2000	2001	2002	2003	2004	2005	2006	2007	2008	
Bahrain	1 553	1 910	2 045	1 979	2 035	2 114	2 215	2 222	2 317	2 270	...	البحرين
Egypt	393 250	384 548	404 699	404 531	424 034	440 149	440 790	440 149	451 863	450 596	...	مصر
Iraq	32 464	138 784	179 928	77 727	85 758	95 935	101 820	115 775	...	...	...	العراق
Jordan	9 913	13 018	13 339	16 164	17 220	16 937	17 011	17 883	20 397	20 924	19 403	الأردن
Kuwait	...	3 781	4 227	4 364	4 342	4 424	4 793	4 784	5 247	5 293	...	الكويت
Lebanon	13 263	19 230	19 435	17 568	17 294	17 187	17 774	18 012	18 787	21 092	21 048	لبنان
Oman	2 090	2 164	2 547	2 550	2 564	2 701	2 743	2 849	5 814	6 449	7 415	عمان
Palestine		8 398	9 041	9 177	10 316	10 207	10 029	9 645	9 938	10 203	...	فلسطين
Qatar	871	1 000	1 173	1 210	1 220	1 311	1 341	1 545	1 750	1 776	1 942	قطر
Saudi Arabia	22 396	75 430	86 291	91 319	92 486	89 976	91 243	92 487	93 752	95 166	96 641	المملكة العربية السعودية
Sudan												السودان
Syrian Arab Republic	46 946	52 214	57 759	60 814	62 184	62 880	68 551	73 928	72 534	76 064	...	الجمهورية العربية السورية
United Arab Emirates	3 942	4 779	5 396	5 777	5 994	6 002	6 123	6 361	6 483	7 414	...	الإمارات العربية المتحدة
Yemen	...	5 683	18 441	19 868	21 162	20 559	22 235	19 653	20 607	...	...	اليمن
TOTAL	526 688	710 939	804 321	713 048	746 609	770 382	786 668	805 293	709 489	697 247	146 449	المجموع

جدول 55: معدل الوفيات الخام لكل ألف من الولادات في بلدان الإسكوا 1990-2008
Table 55: Crude Death Rate (per'000) Live Births in ESCWA Countries 1990-2008

	1990	1995	2000	2001	2002	2003	2004	2005	2006	2007	2008	
Bahrain	3.2	3.3	3.1	3.1	3.0	3.0	3.1	3.1	3.1	3.0	...	البحرين
Egypt	6.8	6.0	5.8	5.7	5.8	5.9	5.8	5.7	5.7	5.6	...	مصر
Iraq	1.8	6.6	7.3	3.1	3.3	3.6	3.7	4.1	...	...	...	العراق
Jordan	3.0	3.0	2.7	3.3	3.4	3.2	3.2	3.2	3.5	3.5	3.2	الأردن
Kuwait	...	2.2	1.9	1.9	1.8	1.7	1.8	1.8	1.9	1.9	...	الكويت
Lebanon	4.5	5.5	5.2	4.6	4.4	4.3	4.3	4.4	4.6	5.1	5.0	لبنان
Oman	1.1	1.0	1.1	1.0	1.0	1.1	1.1	1.1	2.2	2.4	2.7	عمان
Palestine		3.2	2.9	2.8	3.0	2.9	2.8	2.6	2.6	2.5	...	فلسطين
Qatar	1.9	1.9	1.9	1.9	1.8	1.8	1.7	1.7	1.7	1.6	1.5	قطر
Saudi Arabia	1.4	4.1	4.1	4.3	4.2	4.0	4.0	4.0	3.9	3.9	3.8	المملكة العربية السعودية
Sudan												السودان
Syrian Arab Republic	3.7	3.6	3.5	3.5	3.6	3.6	3.7	3.7	3.7	3.7	3.7	الجمهورية العربية السورية
United Arab Emirates	2.1	2.0	1.7	1.7	1.7	1.7	1.6	1.6	1.5	1.7	...	الإمارات العربية المتحدة
Yemen	...	0.4	1.0	1.1	1.1	1.0	1.1	1.1	1.0	1.0	...	اليمن

Calculations are made on the basis of population estimates taken from the
United Nations World Population Prospects: the 2008 Revision

حُسبت المعدلات استنادا إلى تقديرات السكان الواردة في منشور الأمم المتحدة "التوقعات السكانية في العالم: تنقيح عام 2008"

2008-1990 ﺍﻹﺴﻜﻭﺍ ﺒﻠﺩﺍﻥ ﻓﻲ ﺍﻟﺴﻜﺎﻥ ﻤﻥ ﻤﺎﺌﺔ ﻟﻜل ﺍﻟﻁﺒﻴﻌﻴﺔ ﺍﻟﺯﻴﺎﺩﺓ ﻤﻌﺩل :56ﺠﺩﻭل

Table 56: Rate of Natural Increase (per '00) population in ESCWA Countries 1990-2008

	1990	1995	2000	2001	2002	2003	2004	2005	2006	2007	2008	
Bahrain	2.4	2.0	1.8	1.7	1.7	1.8	1.8	1.8	1.7	1.8	...	البحرين
Egypt	2.2	1.9	1.9	1.9	1.8	1.8	1.8	1.8	1.8	1.9	...	مصر
Iraq	3.5	1.5	1.2	2.5	2.5	2.2	2.7	2.8	...	...	...	العراق
Jordan	3.1	3.0	2.3	2.5	2.5	2.5	2.5	2.4	2.5	2.8	2.6	الأردن
Kuwait	...	2.1	1.7	1.6	1.6	1.6	1.6	1.7	1.7	1.7	...	الكويت
Lebanon	1.9	2.1	1.8	1.7	1.5	1.4	1.4	1.4	1.3	1.4	1.5	لبنان
Oman	2.7	2.6	1.6	1.5	1.5	1.5	1.5	1.5	1.6	1.7	1.8	عمان
Palestine	...	3.7	3.0	2.9	2.8	2.7	2.8	2.7	2.5	2.6	...	فلسطين
Qatar	2.2	1.8	1.6	1.7	1.6	1.6	1.5	1.3	1.2	1.2	1.2	قطر
Saudi Arabia	2.1	2.6	2.2	2.2	2.1	2.1	2.1	2.1	2.1	2.0	2.0	المملكة العربية السعودية
Sudan	...	...	...	...	...	...	...	...	...	...	...	السودان
Syrian Arab Republic	2.9	2.9	2.7	2.7	2.9	3.0	2.9	2.9	3.0	3.2	...	الجمهورية العربية السورية
United Arab Emirates	2.6	1.8	1.5	1.5	1.5	1.5	1.4	1.4	1.3	1.4	...	الإمارات العربية المتحدة
Yemen	...	0.6	1.3	1.3	0.9	0.6	0.6	0.6	1.2	...	...	اليمن

Calculations are mades on the basis of population estimates taken from
the United Nations World Population Prospects: the 2008 Revision

ﺍﻟﻤﺘﺤﺩﺓ ﺍﻷﻤﻡ ﻤﻨﺸﻭﺭ ﻓﻲ ﺍﻟﻭﺍﺭﺩﺓ ﺍﻟﺴﻜﺎﻥ ﺘﻘﺩﻴﺭﺍﺕ ﺇﻟﻰ ﺍﺴﺘﻨﺎﺩﺍ ﺍﻟﻤﻌﺩﻻﺕ ﺤﺴﺒﺕ
"2008 ﻋﺎﻡ ﺘﻨﻘﻴﺢ :ﺍﻟﻌﺎﻟﻡ ﻓﻲ ﺍﻟﺴﻜﺎﻨﻴﺔ ﺍﻟﺘﻭﻗﻌﺎﺕ"

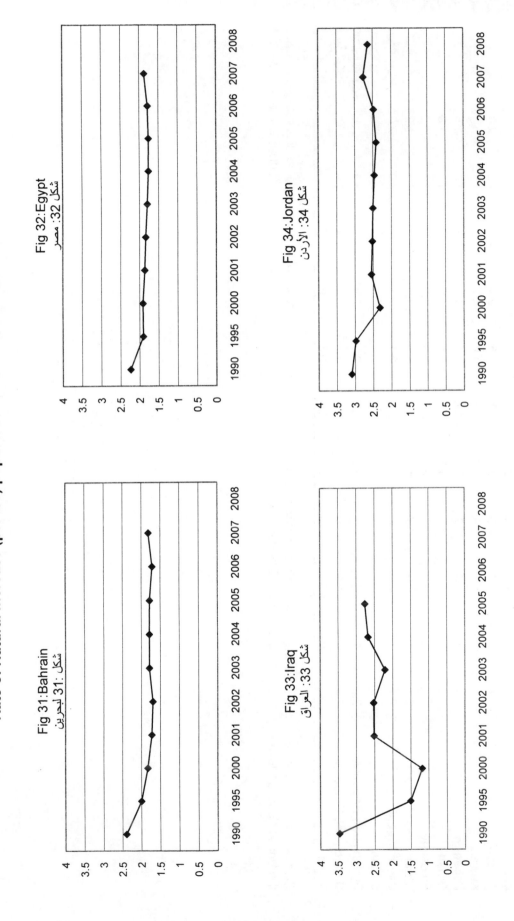

معدل الزيادة الطبيعية لكل مائة من السكان في بلدان الإسكوا 1990-2008
Rate of Natural Increase (per '00) population in ESCWA Countries 1990-2008

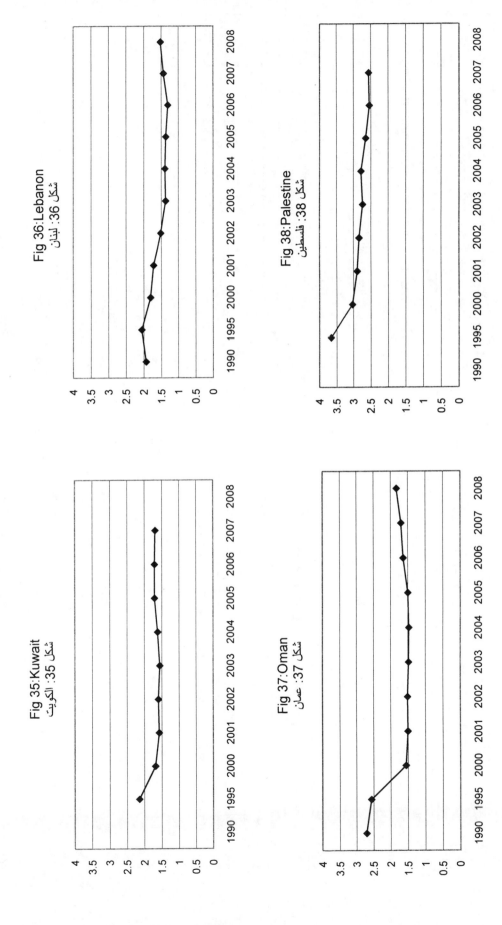

معدل الزيادة الطبيعية لكل مائة من السكان في بلدان الإسكوا (تابع)
Rate of Natural Increase (per'00) population in ESCWA Countries 1990-2008 (cont'd)

Fig 36:Lebanon
شكل 36: لبنان

Fig 38:Palestine
شكل 38: فلسطين

Fig 35:Kuwait
شكل 35: الكويت

Fig 37:Oman
شكل 37: عمان

معدل الزيادة الطبيعية لكل مائة من السكان في بلدان الإسكوا (تابع)

Rate of Natural Increase (per'00) population in ESCWA Countries 1990-2008 (cont'd)

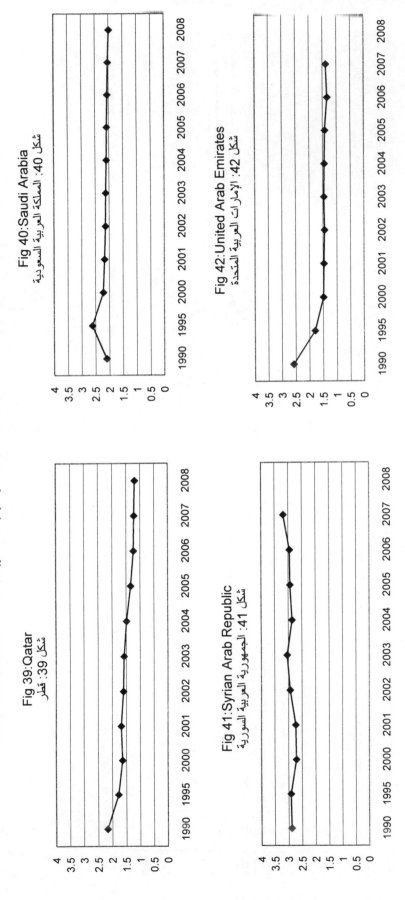

Fig 39:Qatar
شكل 39: قطر

Fig 40:Saudi Arabia
شكل 40: المملكة العربية السعودية

Fig 41:Syrian Arab Republic
شكل 41: الجمهورية العربية السورية

Fig 42:United Arab Emirates
شكل 42: الإمارات العربية المتحدة

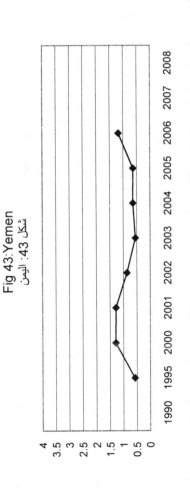

Fig 43:Yemen
شكل 43: اليمن

جدول 57: وفيات الاجنة في بلدان الإسكوا 1990-2008
Table 57: Foetal deaths in ESCWA countries 1990-2008

Country	1990	1995	2000	2001	2002	2003	2004	2005	2006	2007	2008	
Bahrain	...	...	...	...	...	...	...	...	...	...	...	البحرين
Egypt	...	...	5 209	5 393	4 745	4 605	4 201	4 216	4 557	...	...	مصر
Iraq				...		...				...	...	العراق
Jordan	...	...	...	...	...	...	...	...	...	...	...	الأردن
Kuwait	...	...	269	286	325	307	355	375	347	374	...	الكويت
Lebanon										...	...	لبنان
Oman	573	376	388	365	376	381	346	387	367	449	454	عمان
Palestine				...		...				...	...	فلسطين
Qatar			76	75	62	81	64	97	79	95	133	قطر
Saudi Arabia	...	...	...	...	...	...	...	...	...			المملكة العربية السعودية
Sudan	...	...	...	...	...	...	...	...	...			السودان
Syrian Arab Republic	...	...	...	...	...	...	...	...	...			الجمهورية العربية السورية
United Arab Emirates	...	...	...	...	...	...	...	...	...			الإمارات العربية المتحدة
Yemen	...	...	...	...	...	...	...	...	...			اليمن
TOTAL	573	376	5 942	6 119	5 508	5 374	4 966	5 075	5 350	918	587	المجموع

جدول 58: معدل وفيات الاجنة لكل الف من الولادات الحية في بلدان الإسكوا 1990-2008
Table 58: Foetal Mortality Rate (per '000) Live Births in ESCWA countries 1990-2008

Country	1990	1995	2000	2001	2002	2003	2004	2005	2006	2007	2008	
Bahrain	...	...	...	...	...	...	...	...	...	...	...	البحرين
Egypt	...	...	3.0	3.1	2.7	2.6	2.4	2.3	2.5	...	...	مصر
Iraq				...		...				...	...	العراق
Jordan	...	...	...	...	...	...	...	...	...	...	...	الأردن
Kuwait	...	...	6.4	6.9	7.5	7.0	7.5	7.4	6.6	7.0	...	الكويت
Lebanon										...	...	لبنان
Oman	11.0	6.5	9.7	9.3	9.3	9.5	8.5	9.2	7.4	8.5	7.8	عمان
Palestine				...		...				...	...	فلسطين
Qatar			6.8	6.2	5.1	6.3	4.9	7.2	5.6	6.1	7.7	قطر
Saudi Arabia	...	...	...	...	...	...	...	...	...			المملكة العربية السعودية
Sudan	...	...	...	...	...	...	...	...	...			السودان
Syrian Arab Republic	...	...	...	...	...	...	...	...	...			الجمهورية العربية السورية
United Arab Emirates	...	...	...	...	...	...	...	...	...			الإمارات العربية المتحدة
Yemen	...	...	...	...	...	...	...	...	...			اليمن

Calculations are mades on the basis of registered live births

احتسبت المعدلات استناداً إلى بيانات الولادات الحية المسجلة

جدول 59: وفيات الرضّع في بلدان الإسكوا 1990-2008
Table 59: Infant deaths in ESCWA countries 1990-2008

	1990	1995	2000	2001	2002	2003	2004	2005	2006	2007	2008	
Bahrain	272	254	117	117	94	107	135	134	115	133	127	البحرين
Egypt	63 813	47 734	55 214	49 149	37 904	38 859	40 177	39 146	35 952	34 612	...	مصر
Iraq	14 998	...	...	...	12 447	9 638	10 972	12 460	...	...	...	العراق
Jordan	...	...	...	...	...	...	...	...	...	...	...	الأردن
Kuwait	...	450	379	420	418	412	422	420	456	449	...	الكويت
Lebanon	...	...	...	...	...	...	...	...	...	...	...	لبنان
Oman	681	457	369	335	332	335	336	315	381	471	459	عمان
Palestine	...	1 654	1 056	1 138	1 126	1 150	1 103	1 057	906	595	...	فلسطين
Qatar	142	111	132	111	107	127	113	110	114	117	132	قطر
Saudi Arabia	8 436	13 468	11 489	11 377	11 299	11 224	11 164	11 078	10 954	10 782	10 576	المملكة العربية السعودية
Sudan	...	...	...	...	...	...	...	...	...	...	...	السودان
Syrian Arab Republic	...	...	...	...	...	...	...	...	...	...	...	الجمهورية العربية السورية
United Arab Emirates	556	467	443	499	472	477	550	500	447	528	...	الإمارات العربية المتحدة
Yemen	...	...	...	...	...	...	...	...	...	...	...	اليمن
TOTAL	88 898	64 595	69 199	63 146	64 199	62 329	64 972	65 220	49 325	47 687	11 294	المجموع

جدول 60: معدل وفيات الرضّع لكل ألف من الولادات الحية في بلدان الإسكوا 1990-2008
Table 60: Infant Mortality Rate (per'000) Live Births in ESCWA countries 1990-2008

	1990	1995	2000	2001	2002	2003	2004	2005	2006	2007	2008	
Bahrain	20.3	18.8	8.4	8.7	6.9	7.3	9.0	8.8	7.6	8.3	7.5	البحرين
Egypt	37.8	29.7	31.5	28.2	21.5	21.9	22.6	21.7	19.4	17.8	...	مصر
Iraq	22.7	...	...	...	16.7	13.9	13.1	13.9	...	...	...	العراق
Jordan	...	...	...	...	...	...	...	...	...	...	...	الأردن
Kuwait	...	11.0	9.1	10.2	9.6	9.4	8.9	8.2	8.6	8.4	...	الكويت
Lebanon	...	...	...	...	...	...	...	...	...	...	...	لبنان
Oman	13.1	7.9	9.2	8.5	8.3	8.4	8.3	7.5	7.7	9.0	7.9	عمان
Palestine	...	15.8	10.1	11.0	10.6	10.8	9.9	9.7	8.3	5.3	...	فلسطين
Qatar	12.9	10.7	11.7	9.2	8.8	9.9	8.6	8.2	8.1	7.5	7.7	قطر
Saudi Arabia	23.1	24.4	21.0	20.5	20.1	19.8	19.4	19.0	18.6	18.1	17.7	المملكة العربية السعودية
Sudan	...	...	...	...	...	...	...	...	...	...	...	السودان
Syrian Arab Republic	...	...	...	...	...	...	...	...	...	...	...	الجمهورية العربية السورية
United Arab Emirates	10.6	9.6	8.3	8.9	8.1	7.8	8.7	7.7	7.1	7.8	...	الإمارات العربية المتحدة
Yemen	...	...	...	...	...	...	...	...	...	...	...	اليمن

Calculations are mades on the basis of registered live births
احتُسبت المعدلات استناداً إلى بيانات الولادات الحية المسجلة

جدول 61: الإسكو الأطفال في بلدان وفيات
Table 61: child deaths in ESCWA countries 1990-2008

	1990	1995	2000	2001	2002	2003	2004	2005	2006	2007	2008	
Bahrain	296	285	154	162	121	138	161	165	152	165	...	البحرين
Egypt	94 392	66 548	67 637	61 609	49 268	51 909	51 966	46 881	46 978	44 163	...	مصر
Iraq	8 903	55 823	81 804	...	...	...	...	...	...	...	...	العراق
Jordan				...								الاردن
Kuwait		529	492	507	492	497	510	504	533	533		الكويت
Lebanon												لبنان
Oman	61	60	59	57	71	51	55	63	57	127	119	عمان
Palestine	...	2 096	1 407	1 504	1 453	1 542	1 433	1 384	1 249	1 074	...	فلسطين
Qatar	184	137	147	137	124	160	137	140	151	142	164	قطر
Saudi Arabia	10 031	15 900	13 857	13 662	13 470	13 283	13 099	12 974	12 796	12 571	12 309	المملكة العربية السعودية
Sudan												السودان
Syrian Arab Republic												الجمهورية العربية السورية
United Arab Emirates	742	647	580	605	616	...	...	638	545	648	...	الإمارات العربية المتحدة
Yemen												اليمن
TOTAL	114 609	142 025	166 137	78 243	65 615	67 580	67 361	62 749	62 461	59 423	12 592	المجموع

جدول 62: الإسكو بلدان في الحية الولادات من ألف لكل الأطفال وفيات معدل
Table 62: Child Mortality Rate (per'000) Live Births in ESCWA countries 1990-2008

	1990	1995	2000	2001	2002	2003	2004	2005	2006	2007	2008	
Bahrain	22.1	21.1	11.0	12.0	8.9	9.5	10.8	10.9	10.1	10.3	...	البحرين
Egypt	56.0	41.5	38.6	35.4	27.9	29.2	29.2	26.0	25.3	22.7	...	مصر
Iraq	13.5	122.5	173.4	...	...	...	...	...	...	...	...	العراق
Jordan												الاردن
Kuwait		13.0	11.8	12.3	11.3	11.3	10.8	9.9	10.1	9.9	...	الكويت
Lebanon												لبنان
Oman	1.2	1.0	1.5	1.5	1.8	1.3	1.4	1.5	1.2	2.4	2.0	عمان
Palestine	...	20.1	13.4	14.5	13.6	14.5	12.9	12.6	11.5	9.5	...	فلسطين
Qatar	16.7	13.2	13.1	11.3	10.2	12.4	10.4	10.4	10.7	9.1	9.5	قطر
Saudi Arabia	27.5	28.8	25.3	24.7	24.0	23.4	22.8	22.3	21.7	21.1	20.6	المملكة العربية السعودية
Sudan												السودان
Syrian Arab Republic												الجمهورية العربية السورية
United Arab Emirates	14.2	13.3	10.8	10.8	10.6	...	...	9.9	8.7	9.6	...	الإمارات العربية المتحدة
Yemen												اليمن

Calculations are mades on the basis of registered live births   المحددات استنادا إلى بيانات الولادات الحية المسجلة

الوفيات، وفيات الرضع ووفيات الأطفال في بلدان الإسكوا حسب توفر البيانات

Deaths, infant deaths, child deaths in ESCWA countries according to data availability

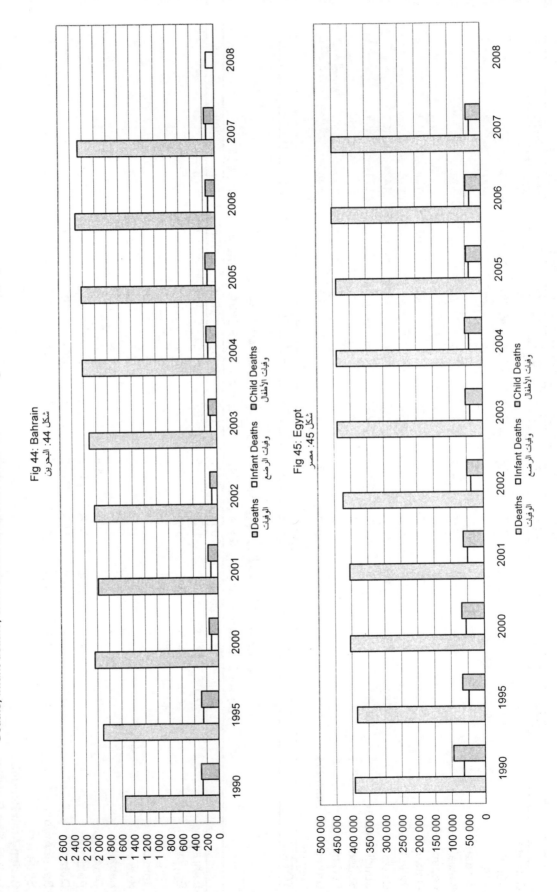

Fig 44: Bahrain
شكل 44: البحرين

■Deaths ■Infant Deaths ■Child Deaths
الوفيات وفيات الرضع وفيات الأطفال

Fig 45: Egypt
شكل 45: مصر

■Deaths ■Infant Deaths ■Child Deaths
الوفيات وفيات الرضع وفيات الأطفال

الوفيات، وفيات الرضّع ووفيات الأطفال في بلدان الإسكوا حسب توفر البيانات (تابع)

Deaths, infant deaths, child deaths in ESCWA countries according to data availability (cont'd)

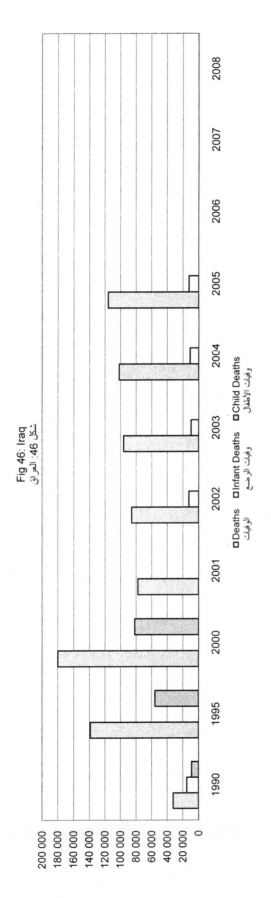

Fig 46: Iraq
شكل 46: العراق

□Deaths   □Infant Deaths   ■Child Deaths
الوفيات   وفيات الرضّع   وفيات الأطفال

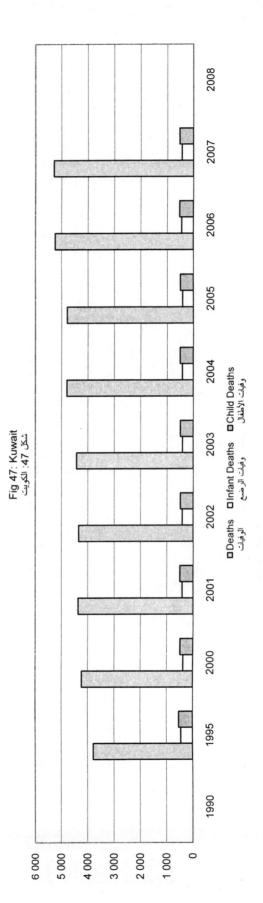

Fig 47: Kuwait
شكل 47: الكويت

□Deaths   □Infant Deaths   ■Child Deaths
الوفيات   وفيات الرضّع   وفيات الأطفال

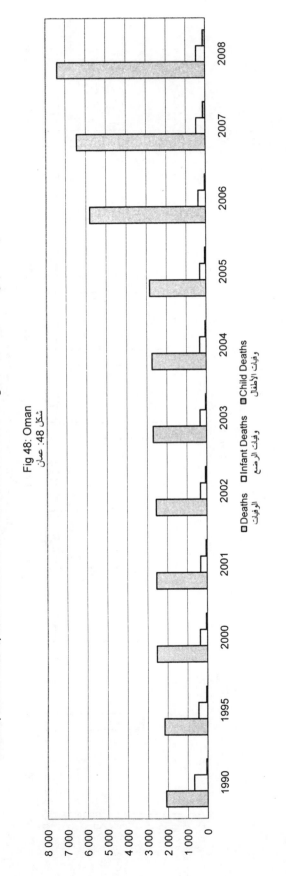

الوفيات، وفيات الرضع ووفيات الأطفال في بلدان الإسكوا حسب توفر البيانات (تابع)

Deaths, infant deaths, child deaths in ESCWA countries according to data availability (cont'd)

Fig 48: Oman
شكل 48: عمان

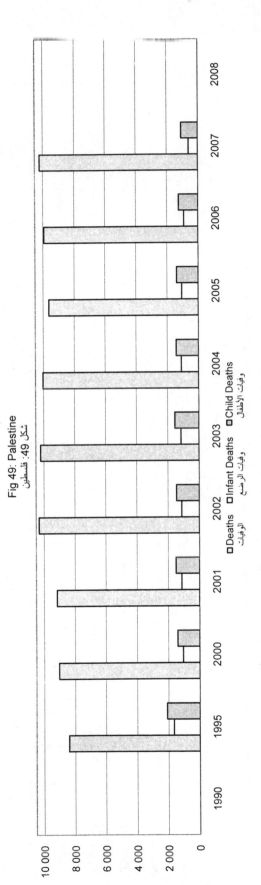

Fig 49: Palestine
شكل 49: فلسطين

الوفيات، وفيات الرضع ووفيات الأطفال في بلدان الإسكوا حسب توفر البيانات (تابع)

Deaths, infant deaths, child deaths in ESCWA countries according to data availability (cont'd)

Fig 50:Qatar
شكل 50: قطر

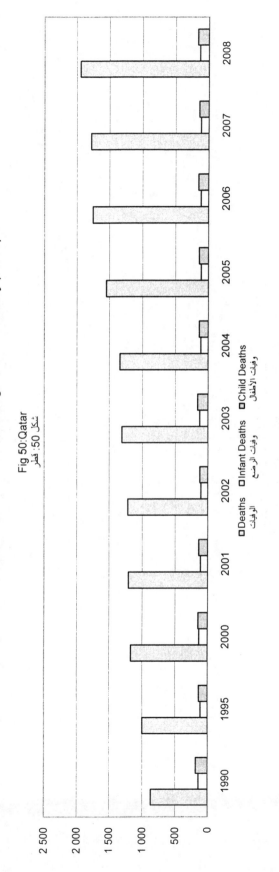

Fig 51: Saudi Arabia
شكل 51: المملكة العربية السعودية

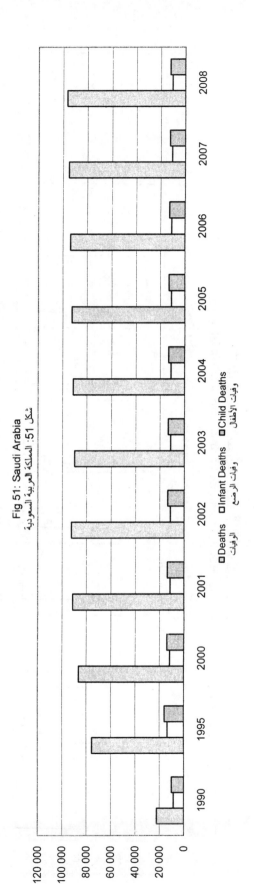

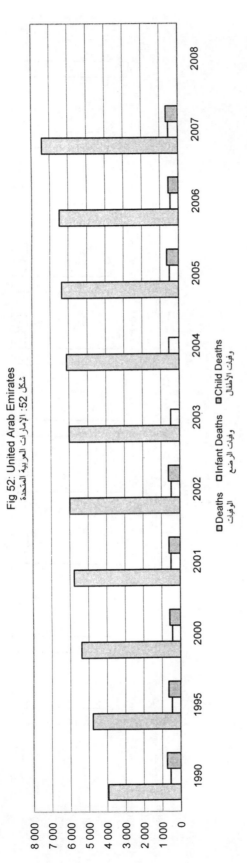

الوفيات، وفيات الرضّع ووفيات الأطفال في بلدان الإسكوا حسب توفر البيانات (تابع)

Deaths, infant deaths, child deaths in ESCWA countries according to data availability (cont'd)

Fig 52: United Arab Emirates
شكل 52: الإمارات العربية المتحدة

جدول 63: معدل الخصوبة العام، ومعدل الخصوبة الكلي لدى المراهقات ومعدل الإحلال الإجمالي، ومتوسط عمر المرأة عند الإنجاب منذ عام 1990

Table 63: General Fertility, Total Fertility, Adolescent Fertility, Gross Reproduction Rates, and Mean Age of Childbearing since 1990

	متوسط عمر المرأة عند الإنجاب Mean Age of Childbearing	معدل الإحلال الإجمالي (لكل امرأة) Gross Reproduction Rate (per women)	معدل الخصوبة لدى المراهقات (19-15) سنة (بالألف) Adolescent Fertility Rate (15-19 yrs) (per '000)	معدل الخصوبة الكلية (لكل امرأة) Total Fertility Rate (per women)	معدل الخصوبة العام General Fertility Rate	المواليد الإناث Female Births	المواليد الأحياء Live Births	السكان النساء (49-15) سنة Female Population (15-49 yrs)
BAHRAIN البحرين								
2008	29.7	1.3	13.4	2.7	85.3	8 345	17 022	199 508
2007	29.8	1.3	13.9	2.6	82.8	7 877	16 062	193 953
2006	29.7	1.2	14.4	2.5	79.8	7 406	15 053	188 552
2005	29.6	1.3	17.1	2.6	82.8	7 430	15 198	183 495
2004	29.6	1.4	19.2	2.7	83.7	7 469	14 968	178 893
2003	29.7	1.3	19.6	2.6	83.4	7 256	14 560	174 675
2002	30.3	1.2	13.2	2.5	79.6	6 623	13 576	170 604
2001	30.3	1.2	12.0	2.6	81.0	6 536	13 468	166 337
2000	30.5	1.3	14.1	2.7	86.3	6 841	13 947	161 644
1995	30.2	1.5	19.6	3.1	100.4	6 545	13 481	134 217
1990	30.7	1.7	24.2	3.5	118.0	6 526	13 370	113 319
EGYPT مصر								
2007	28.8	1.4	26.0	2.9	92.0	951 160	1949 569	21191 600
2006	28.9	1.4	23.2	2.9	89.2	902 661	1853 746	20780 440
2005	28.7	1.4	20.8	2.9	88.6	881 835	1800 972	20318 862
2004	29.0	1.5	20.2	2.9	89.9	877 341	1779 500	19798 925
2003	29.1	1.5	20.3	3.1	92.4	877 320	1777 418	19229 931
2002	29.0	1.5	17.0	3.1	94.8	861 038	1766 591	18636 833
2001	28.9	1.5	17.1	3.2	96.4	846 358	1741 308	18054 699
2000	29.1	1.6	15.8	3.3	100.1	847 098	1751 854	17508 930
1995	29.7	1.7	12.4	3.5	105.1	769 150	1604 835	15270 496
1990	30.7	2.1	13.6	4.3	128.0	815 564	1686 877	13180 137
IRAQ العراق								
2000	30.6	1.2	16.4	2.7	81.4	216 348	471 886	5799 789
1995	30.8	1.6	27.3	3.2	94.6	224 347	455 727	4817 787
1990	35.7	3.6	0.5	7.3	167.6	329 978	670 385	3999 852

جدول 63: معدل الخصوبة العام، ومعدل الخصوبة الكلي لدى المراهقات ومعدل الإحلال الإجمالي، ومتوسط عمر المرأة عند الإنجاب منذ عام 1990

Table 63: General Fertility, Total Fertility, Adolescent Fertility, Gross Reproduction Rates, and Mean Age of Childbearing since 1990

	Female Population (15-49 yrs)	Live Births	Female Births	General Fertility Rate	Total Fertility Rate (per women)	Adolescent Fertility Rate (15-19 yrs) (per '000)	Gross Reproduction Rate (per women)	Mean Age of Childbearing	
KUWAIT									الكويت
	712 100	53 587	26 129	75.3	2.3	13.2	1.1	29.6	2007
	692 311	52 759	25 836	76.2	2.3	14.3	1.1	29.6	2006
	669 739	50 941	25 019	76.1	2.3	14.2	1.1	29.7	2005
	644 617	47 274	23 039	73.3	2.2	15.2	1.1	29.6	2004
	617 500	43 982	21 569	71.2	2.2	16.3	1.1	29.5	2003
	588 648	43 490	21 356	73.9	2.2	16.3	1.1	29.5	2002
	558 416	41 342	20 316	74.0	2.2	17.5	1.1	29.4	2001
	527 415	41 843	20 511	79.3	2.4	17.3	1.2	29.6	2000
	402 253	41 169	20 216	102.3	3.0	32.7	1.5	29.4	1995
	449 731	20 609	10 013	45.8	1.3	10.5	0.6	29.0	1991
OMAN									عمان
	613 738	58 250	28 313	94.9	2.8	8.4	1.4	30.2	2007
	594 819	52 619	25 829	88.5	2.7	8.0	1.3	30.2	2007
	576 084	49 499	24 086	85.9	2.6	7.7	1.3	30.2	2007
QATAR									قطر
	193 757	17 210	8 507	88.8	2.7	15.2	1.3	30.4	2007
	173 804	15 681	7 625	90.2	2.8	15.6	1.3	30.4	2007
	155 759	14 120	6 924	90.7	2.8	16.7	1.4	30.3	2006
	141 924	13 401	6 562	94.4	3.0	16.5	1.5	30.2	2005
	133 213	13 190	6 388	99.0	3.2	18.5	1.6	30.0	2004
	128 837	12 856	6 292	99.8	3.3	17.9	1.6	29.7	2003
	127 305	12 200	5 939	95.8	3.2	20.3	1.6	29.6	2002
	130 583	12 118	5 932	92.8	3.2	17.1	1.5	29.7	2001
	126 331	11 250	5 512	89.1	3.1	16.9	1.5	29.7	2000
	100 712	10 371	5 099	103.0	3.3	28.8	1.6	28.9	1995
	81 540	11 022	5 392	135.2	4.4	55.3	2.1	28.3	1990

جدول 63: معدل الخصوبة العام، ومعدل الخصوبة الكلي لدى المراهقات، ومعدل الإحلال الإجمالي، ومتوسط عمر المرأة عند الإنجاب منذ عام 1990

Table 63: General Fertility, Total Fertility, Adolescent Fertility, Gross Reproduction Rates, and Mean Age of Childbearing since 1990

	Female Population (15-49 yrs) السكان النساء (15-49 سنة)	Live Births المواليد الأحياء	Female Births المواليد الإناث	General Fertility Rate معدل الخصوبة العام	Total Fertility Rate (per women) معدل الخصوبة الكلية (لكل امرأة)	Adolescent Fertility Rate (15-19 yrs) (per '000) معدل الخصوبة لدى المراهقات (15-19 سنة) (بالألف)	Gross Reproduction Rate (per women) معدل الإحلال الإجمالي (لكل امرأة)	Mean Age of Childbearing متوسط عمر المرأة عند الإنجاب	الإمارات العربية المتحدة
UNITED ARAB EMIRATES									
2003	756 091	61 165	29 924	80.9	2.4	23.3	1.2	30.9	**2003**
2002	709 225	58 070	28 562	81.9	2.5	21.5	1.2	30.8	**2002**
2001	663 555	56 136	27 518	84.6	2.6	21.5	1.3	30.9	**2001**
2000	620 907	53 686	26 046	86.5	2.7	21.9	1.3	31.1	**2000**
1995	455 264	48 567	23 816	106.7	3.3	37.2	1.6	30.4	**1995**
1990	336 056	52 264	25 394	155.5	4.8	53.5	2.3	29.3	**1990**

Calculations are made on the basis of registered live births and population estimates taken
from the United Nations World Population Prospects: the 2008 Revision

احتسبت المعدلات استناداً إلى بيانات الولادات الحية المسجلة و تقديرات السكان الواردة في منشور الأمم
المتحدة

-75-

2008-1990 معدل الخصوبة الكلي لكل امرأة حسب توفر البيانات

Fig 53: Total Fertility Rate per woman according to data availability 1990-2008

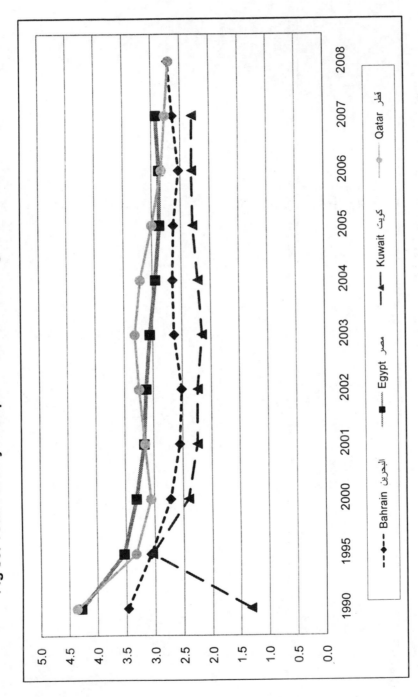

Table 64: Registered Deaths by Cause: Crude Rates and Per Cent

BAHRAIN 2007 / البحرين

cause of death (1) سبب الوفاة (1)	Grand Total المجموع العام			Nationals المواطنون			Non-Nationals غير مواطنين			Rate (per 100 thousand population) المعدل الخام (لكل مائة ألف من السكان)			per cent النسبة في السنة		
	Total مجموع	Men رجال	Women نساء	Total مجموع	Men رجال	Women نساء	Total مجموع	Men رجال	Women نساء	Total مجموع	Men رجال	Women نساء	Total مجموع	Men رجال	Women نساء
1	69	38	31	53	26	27	16	12	4	9.1	8.7	9.6	3.0	2.7	3.7
2	240	144	96	213	127	86	27	17	10	31.6	33.0	29.7	10.6	10.1	11.3
3	250	142	108	226	123	103	24	19	5	32.9	32.5	33.4	11.0	10.0	12.8
4	36	18	18	35	17	18	1	1	-	4.7	4.1	5.6	1.6	1.3	2.1
5	6	5	1	4	3	1	2	2	-	0.8	1.1	0.3	0.3	0.4	0.1
6	49	25	24	41	20	21	8	5	3	6.5	5.7	7.4	2.2	1.8	2.8
7	447	259	188	365	197	168	82	62	20	58.8	59.3	58.2	19.7	18.2	22.2
8	173	105	68	153	91	62	20	14	6	22.8	24.1	21.0	7.6	7.4	8.0
9	61	33	28	53	29	24	8	4	4	8.0	7.6	8.7	2.7	2.3	3.3
10	104	52	52	97	46	51	7	6	1	13.7	11.9	16.1	4.6	3.7	6.1
11	3	-	3	3	-	3	-	-	-	0.4	-	0.9	0.1	-	0.4
12	23	10	13	23	10	13	-	-	-	3.0	2.3	4.0	1.0	0.7	1.5
13	8	3	5	7	2	5	1	1	-	1.1	0.7	1.5	0.4	0.2	0.6
14	60	35	25	41	22	19	19	13	6	7.9	8.0	7.7	2.6	2.5	3.0
15	50	24	26	38	18	20	12	6	6	6.6	5.5	8.0	2.2	1.7	3.1
16	466	331	135	336	221	115	130	110	20	61.4	75.8	41.8	20.5	23.3	15.9
17	-	-	-	-	-	-	-	-	-	-	-	-	-	-	-
18	-	-	-	-	-	-	-	-	-	-	-	-	-	-	-
19	-	-	-	-	-	-	-	-	-	-	-	-	-	-	-
20	-	-	-	-	-	-	-	-	-	-	-	-	-	-	-
21	225	199	26	86	71	15	-	128	11	29.6	45.6	8.0	9.9	14.0	3.1
22	-	-	-	-	-	-	-	-	-	-	-	-	-	-	-
Total المجموع	**2 270**	**1 423**	**847**	**1 774**	**1 023**	**751**	**496**	**400**	**96**	**298.9**	**326.1**	**262.1**	**100.0**	**100.0**	**100.0**

(1) Causes of death given in annex 1

Calculations are made on the basis of population estimates taken from the United Nations World Population Prospects: the 2008 Revision

(1) أسباب الوفيات في الملحق رقم 1

الحسابات استنادا الى تقديرات السكان الواردة في منشور الأمم المتحدة "التوقعات السكانية في العالم: تنقيح عام 2008"

جدول 64 (تابع) : أسباب الوفيات المسجلة : المعدل الخام والنسبة في المئة

Table 64 (cont'd): Registered Deaths by Cause: Crude Rates and Per Cent

BAHRAIN 2005 cause of death (1)	المجموع العام Grand Total			المواطنون Nationals			غير مواطنين Non-Nationals			المعدل الخام (لكل مائة ألف من السكان) Rate (per 100 thousand population)			النسبة في المئة per cent		
سبب الوفاة (1)	مجموع Total	رجال Men	نساء Women	مجموع Total	رجال Men	نساء Women	مجموع Total	رجال Men	نساء Women	مجموع Total	رجال Men	نساء Women	مجموع Total	رجال Men	نساء Women
1	94	56	38	84	48	36	10	8	2	12.9	13.4	12.3	4.2	4.2	4.3
2	267	133	134	246	122	124	21	11	10	36.7	31.8	43.3	12.0	10.0	15.0
3	233	122	111	206	106	100	27	16	11	32.0	29.2	35.9	10.5	9.2	12.4
4	38	19	19	37	18	19	1	1	-	5.2	4.5	6.1	1.7	1.4	2.1
5	8	8	-	8	8	-	-	-	-	1.1	1.9	-	0.4	0.6	-
6	48	33	15	41	26	15	7	7	-	6.6	7.9	4.9	2.2	2.5	1.7
7	434	252	182	359	188	171	75	64	11	59.7	60.2	58.8	19.5	19.0	20.4
8	143	84	59	125	72	53	18	12	6	19.7	20.1	19.1	6.4	6.3	6.6
9	65	35	30	55	28	27	10	7	3	8.9	8.4	9.7	2.9	2.6	3.4
10	91	45	46	82	39	43	9	6	3	12.5	10.8	14.9	4.1	3.4	5.2
11	-	-	-	-	-	-	-	-	-	-	-	-	-	-	-
12	49	26	23	47	25	22	2	1	1	6.7	6.2	7.4	2.2	2.0	2.6
13	4	1	3	2	-	2	2	1	1	0.5	0.2	1.0	0.2	0.1	0.3
14	47	23	24	38	17	21	9	6	3	6.5	5.5	7.8	2.1	1.7	2.7
15	62	36	26	52	31	21	10	5	5	8.5	8.6	8.4	2.8	2.7	2.9
16	429	285	144	323	192	131	106	93	13	59.0	68.1	46.6	19.3	21.5	16.1
17	205	166	39	95	71	24	110	95	15	28.2	39.7	12.6	9.2	12.5	4.4
18	-	-	-	-	-	-	-	-	-	-	-	-	-	-	-
المجموع Total	2 222	1 324	893	1 800	991	809	417	333	84	305.4	316.5	288.7	100.0	100.0	100.0

(1) Causes of death given in annex 1

Calculations are made on the basis of population estimates taken from the United Nations World Population Prospects: the 2008 Revision

(1) أسباب الوفيات في الملحق رقم 1

حُسبت المعدلات استناداً إلى تقديرات السكان الواردة في منشور الأمم المتحدة "التوقعات السكانية في العالم : تنقيح عام 2008"

جدول 64 (تابع) : أسباب الوفيات المسجلة : المعدل الخام والنسبة في المئة
Table 64 (cont'd): Registered Deaths by Cause: Crude Rates and Per Cent

البحرين BAHRAIN
2000

سبب الوفاة (1) cause of death (1)	المجموع العام Grand Total			المواطنون Nationals			غير مواطنين Non-Nationals			المعدل الخام (لكل مائة ألف من السكان) Rate (per 100 thousand population)			النسبة في المئة percent		
	مجموع Total	رجال Men	نساء Women	مجموع Total	رجال Men	نساء Women	مجموع Total	رجال Men	نساء Women	مجموع Total	رجال Men	نساء Women	مجموع Total	رجال Men	نساء Women
1	85	54	31	71	43	28	14	11	3	13.1	14.4	11.2	4.2	4.4	3.7
2	247	128	119	216	111	105	31	17	14	38.0	34.2	43.1	12.1	10.5	14.4
3	140	79	61	119	64	55	21	15	6	21.5	21.1	22.1	6.8	6.5	7.4
4	19	9	10	17	8	9	2	1	1	2.9	2.4	3.6	0.9	0.7	1.2
5	6	5	1	4	3	1	2	2	-	0.9	1.3	0.4	0.3	0.4	0.1
6	28	17	11	20	11	9	8	6	2	4.3	4.5	4.0	1.4	1.4	1.3
7	536	321	215	420	223	197	116	98	18	82.5	85.8	77.9	26.2	26.4	25.9
8	84	48	36	72	42	30	12	6	6	12.9	12.8	13.0	4.1	3.9	4.3
9	73	37	36	65	30	35	8	7	1	11.2	9.9	13.0	3.6	3.0	4.3
10	54	24	30	52	22	30	2	2	-	8.3	6.4	10.9	2.6	2.0	3.6
11	2	-	2	1	-	1	1	1	-	0.3	-	0.7	0.1	-	0.2
12	39	21	18	4	2	2	35	19	16	6.0	5.6	6.5	1.9	1.7	2.2
13	3	1	2	2	-	2	1	1	-	0.5	0.3	0.7	0.1	0.1	0.2
14	50	28	22	43	24	19	7	4	3	7.7	7.5	8.0	2.4	2.3	2.7
15	58	35	23	41	25	16	17	10	7	8.9	9.4	8.3	2.8	2.9	2.8
16	261	196	65	90	70	20	171	126	45	40.2	52.4	23.6	12.8	16.1	7.8
17	49	41	8	26	21	5	23	20	3	7.5	11.0	2.9	2.4	3.4	1.0
18	311	172	139	278	149	129	33	23	10	47.8	46.0	50.4	15.2	14.1	16.8
المجموع Total	2 045	1 216	829	1 541	848	693	504	368	136	314.6	325.1	300.4	100.0	100.0	100.0

(1) Causes of death given in annex 1

Calculations are mades on the basis of population estimates taken from the United Nations
World Population Prospects: the 2008 Revision

(1) أسباب الوفيات استناداً إلى المعدلات الواردة في الملحق رقم 1

حسبت المعدلات استناداً إلى تقديرات السكان الواردة في منشور الأمم المتحدة
"التوقعات السكانية في العالم، تنقيح عام 2008"

جدول 64 (تابع) : أسباب الوفيات المسجلة : المعدل الخام والنسبة في المئة
Table 64 (cont'd): Registered Deaths by Cause: Crude Rates and Per Cent

EGYPT مصر 2005	المجموع العام Grand Total			المواطنون Nationals			غير مواطنين Non-Nationals			المعدل الخام (لكل مئة ألف من السكان) Rate (per 100 thousand population)			النسبة في المئة percent		
سبب الوفاة (1) cause of death (1)	مجموع Total	رجال Men	نساء Women	مجموع Total	رجال Men	نساء Women	مجموع Total	رجال Men	نساء Women	مجموع Total	رجال Men	نساء Women	مجموع Total	رجال Men	نساء Women
1	14 879	7 897	6 982	...	...	...	...	...	...	19.3	20.3	18.2	3.4	3.3	3.5
2	24 168	13 757	10 411	...	...	...	...	...	...	31.3	35.4	27.2	5.5	5.8	5.1
3	15 977	7 369	8 608	...	...	...	...	...	...	20.7	19.0	22.5	3.6	3.1	4.3
4	1 180	569	611	...	...	...	...	...	...	1.5	1.5	1.6	0.3	0.2	0.3
5	1 037	569	468	...	...	...	...	...	...	1.3	1.5	1.2	0.2	0.2	0.2
6	7 210	3 840	3 370	...	...	...	...	...	...	9.3	9.9	8.8	1.6	1.6	1.7
7	184 007	94 954	89 053	...	...	...	...	...	...	238.5	244.6	232.3	41.8	39.9	44.0
8	33 053	17 311	15 742	...	...	...	...	...	...	42.8	44.6	41.1	7.5	7.3	7.8
9	38 314	24 325	13 989	...	...	...	...	...	...	49.7	62.7	36.5	8.7	10.2	6.9
10	15 971	9 206	6 765	...	...	...	...	...	...	20.7	23.7	17.6	3.6	3.9	3.3
11	1 108	-	1 108	...	...	...	...	...	...	1.4	-	2.9	0.3	-	0.5
12	159	69	90	...	...	...	...	...	...	0.2	0.2	0.2	0.0	0.0	0.0
13	2 219	971	1 248	...	...	...	...	...	...	2.9	2.5	3.3	0.5	0.4	0.6
14	6 354	3 291	3 063	...	...	...	...	...	...	8.2	8.5	8.0	1.4	1.4	1.5
15	9 831	5 607	4 224	...	...	...	...	...	...	12.7	14.4	11.0	2.2	2.4	2.1
16	66 782	35 247	31 535	...	...	...	...	...	...	86.6	90.8	82.3	15.2	14.8	15.6
17	7 503	5 773	1 730	...	...	...	...	...	...	9.7	14.9	4.5	1.7	2.4	0.9
18	10 397	7 112	3 285	...	...	...	...	...	...	13.5	18.3	8.6	2.4	3.0	1.6
19	...	...	...	...	...	...	...	...	...	...	...	...	...	...	...
20	...	...	...	...	...	...	...	...	...	...	...	...	...	...	...
المجموع Total	440 149	237 867	202 282	...	...	...	...	...	...	570.5	612.7	527.7	100.0	100.0	100.0

(1) Causes of death given in annex 1

(1) أسباب الوفيات معطاة في الملحق رقم 1

Calculations are made on the basis of population estimates taken from the United Nations World Population Prospects: the 2008 Revision

اعتمدت المعدلات استناداً إلى تقديرات السكان الواردة في منشور الأمم المتحدة "التوقعات السكانية في العالم: تنقيح عام 2008"

جدول 64 (تابع) : أسباب الوفيات المسجلة : المعدل الخام والنسبة في المئة

Table 64 (cont'd): Registered Deaths by Cause: Crude Rates and Per Cent

EGYPT   مصر

2000

cause of death (1) سبب الوفاة (1)	Grand Total المجموع العام			Nationals المواطنون			Non-Nationals غير مواطنين			Rate (per 100 thousand population) المعدل الخام (لكل مائة ألف من السكان)			percent النسبة في المئة		
	مجموع Total	رجال Men	نساء Women	مجموع Total	رجال Men	نساء Women	مجموع Total	رجال Men	نساء Women	مجموع Total	رجال Men	نساء Women	مجموع Total	رجال Men	نساء Women
1	20 652	11 207	9 445	...	...	...	...	...	...	29.4	31.7	27.1	5.1	5.1	5.2
2	20 496	11 930	8 566	...	...	...	...	...	...	29.2	33.8	24.6	5.1	5.4	4.7
3	11 215	5 030	6 185	...	...	...	...	...	...	16.0	14.2	17.8	2.8	2.3	3.4
4	1 093	591	502	...	...	...	...	...	...	1.6	1.7	1.4	0.3	0.3	0.3
5	479	231	248	...	...	...	...	...	...	0.7	0.7	0.7	0.1	0.1	0.1
6	5 086	2 786	2 300	...	...	...	...	...	...	7.2	7.9	6.6	1.3	1.3	1.3
7	174 511	91 826	82 685	...	...	...	...	...	...	248.7	259.8	237.4	43.1	41.5	45.1
8	37 498	19 739	17 759	...	...	...	...	...	...	53.4	55.9	51.0	9.3	8.9	9.7
9	29 568	18 815	10 753	...	...	...	...	...	...	42.1	53.2	30.9	7.3	8.5	5.9
10	13 522	8 015	5 507	...	...	...	...	...	...	19.3	22.7	15.8	3.3	3.6	3.0
11	532	-	532	...	...	...	...	...	...	0.8	...	1.5	0.1	...	0.3
12	99	58	41	...	...	...	...	...	...	0.1	0.2	0.1	0.0	0.0	0.0
13	316	155	161	...	...	...	...	...	...	0.5	0.4	0.5	0.1	0.1	0.1
14	6 479	3 517	2 962	...	...	...	...	...	...	9.2	10.0	8.5	1.6	1.6	1.6
15	7 992	4 599	3 393	...	...	...	...	...	...	11.4	13.0	9.7	2.0	2.1	1.9
16	57 406	30 072	27 334	...	...	...	...	...	...	81.8	85.1	78.5	14.2	13.6	14.9
17	17 755	12 804	4 951	...	...	...	...	...	...	25.3	36.2	14.2	4.4	5.8	2.7
18	...	...	...	...	...	...	...	...	...	...	...	...	...	...	...
المجموع Total	404 699	221 375	183 324	...	...	...	...	...	...	576.7	626.4	526.3	100.0	100.0	100.0

(1) Causes of death given in annex 1   أسباب الوفيات في الملحق رقم 1 (1)

Calculations are made on the basis of population estimates taken from the United Nations
World Population Prospects: the 2008 Revision

احتسبت المعدلات استنادا إلى تقديرات السكان الواردة في منشور الأمم المتحدة
"توقعات السكان في العالم: تنقيح عام 2008"

جدول 64 (تابع) : أسباب الوفيات المسجلة : المعدل الخام والنسبة في السنة

Table 64 (cont'd): Registered Deaths by Cause: Crude Rates and Per Cent

KUWAIT الكويت

2007

cause of death (1) سبب الوفاة	المجموع العام Grand Total			المواطنون Nationals			غير مواطنين Non-Nationals			المعدل الخام (لكل مئة ألف من السكان) Rate (per 100 thousand population)			النسبة في المئة percent		
	مجموع Total	رجال Men	نساء Women	مجموع Total	رجال Men	نساء Women	مجموع Total	رجال Men	نساء Women	مجموع Total	رجال Men	نساء Women	مجموع Total	رجال Men	نساء Women
1	138	74	64	66	35	31	72	39	33	4.8	4.3	5.6	2.6	2.2	3.3
2	689	368	321	410	208	202	279	160	119	24.2	21.5	28.1	13.0	11.0	16.6
3	209	103	106	142	70	72	67	33	34	7.3	6.0	9.3	3.9	3.1	5.5
4	19	7	12	11	4	7	8	3	5	0.7	0.4	1.1	0.4	0.2	0.6
5	4	2	2	3	2	1	1	-	1	0.1	0.1	0.2	0.1	0.1	0.1
6	79	44	35	51	26	25	28	18	10	2.8	2.6	3.1	1.5	1.3	1.8
7	2 110	1 422	688	1 011	575	436	1 099	847	252	74.0	83.2	60.2	39.9	42.4	35.5
8	307	168	139	184	94	90	123	74	49	10.8	9.8	12.2	5.8	5.0	7.2
9	129	74	55	65	30	35	64	44	20	4.5	4.3	4.8	2.4	2.2	2.8
10	146	76	70	102	52	50	44	24	20	5.1	4.4	6.1	2.8	2.3	3.6
11	1	-	1	-	-	-	1	-	1	0.0	-	0.1	0.0	-	0.1
12	13	2	11	10	1	9	3	1	2	0.5	0.1	1.0	0.2	0.1	0.6
13	1	-	1	-	-	-	1	-	1	0.0	-	0.1	0.0	-	0.1
14	241	123	118	147	80	67	94	43	51	8.5	7.2	10.3	4.6	3.7	6.1
15	200	116	84	129	73	56	71	43	28	7.0	6.8	7.4	3.8	3.5	4.3
16	125	50	75	70	27	43	55	23	32	4.4	2.9	6.6	2.4	1.5	3.9
17	-	-	-	-	-	-	-	-	-	-	-	-	-	-	-
18	-	-	-	-	-	-	-	-	-	-	-	-	-	-	-
19	-	-	-	-	-	-	-	-	-	-	-	-	-	-	-
20	-	-	-	-	-	-	-	-	-	-	-	-	-	-	-
21	882	726	156	324	254	70	558	472	86	30.9	42.5	13.7	16.7	21.6	8.0
22	-	-	-	-	-	-	-	-	-	-	-	-	-	-	-
المجموع Total	5 293	3 355	1 938	2 725	1 531	1 194	2 568	1 824	744	185.6	196.3	169.7	100.0	100.0	100.0

(1) Causes of death given in annex 1

Calculations are made on the basis of population estimates taken from the United Nations
World Population Prospects: the 2008 Revision

(1) أسباب الوفيات مبينة في الملحق رقم 1
احتسبت أسباب الوفيات استنادا إلى تقديرات السكان الواردة في منشور الأمم المتحدة
"التوقعات السكانية في العالم: تنقيح عام 2008"

جدول 64 (تابع) : أسباب الوفيات المسجلة : المعدل الخام والنسبة في المئة

Table 64 (cont'd): Registered Deaths by Cause: Crude Rates and Per Cent

KUWAIT الكويت

2005 سبب الوفاة (1) cause of death (1)	المجموع العام Grand Total			المواطنين Nationals			غير مواطنين Non-Nationals			المعدل الخام (لكل مائة ألف نفر من السكان) Rate (per 100 thousand population)			النسبة في المئة percent		
	مجموع Total	رجال Men	نساء Women	مجموع Total	رجال Men	نساء Women	مجموع Total	رجال Men	نساء Women	مجموع Total	رجال Men	نساء Women	مجموع Total	رجال Men	نساء Women
1	126	74	52	61	36	25	65	38	27	4.7	4.5	4.9	2.6	2.4	3.2
2	578	315	263	334	160	174	244	155	89	21.4	19.3	24.5	12.1	10.0	16.0
3	205	118	87	123	67	56	82	51	31	7.6	7.2	8.1	4.3	3.8	5.3
4	17	9	8	11	5	6	6	4	2	0.6	0.6	0.7	0.4	0.3	0.5
5	5	3	2	4	2	2	1	1	-	0.2	0.2	0.2	0.1	0.1	0.1
6	62	41	21	40	25	15	22	16	6	2.3	2.5	2.0	1.3	1.3	1.3
7	1 952	1 336	616	944	569	375	1 008	767	241	72.3	82.0	57.5	40.8	42.6	37.4
8	244	129	115	162	86	76	82	43	39	9.0	7.9	10.7	5.1	4.1	7.0
9	136	76	60	72	33	39	64	43	21	5.0	4.7	5.6	2.8	2.4	3.6
10	82	48	34	60	35	25	22	13	9	3.0	2.9	3.2	1.7	1.5	2.1
11	2	-	2	1	-	1	1	-	1	0.1	-	0.2	0.0	-	0.1
12	10	3	7	6	2	4	4	1	3	0.4	0.2	0.7	0.2	0.1	0.4
13	3	2	1	-	-	-	3	2	1	0.1	0.1	0.1	0.1	0.1	0.1
14	240	130	110	133	69	64	107	61	46	8.9	8.0	10.3	5.0	4.1	6.7
15	167	87	80	100	57	43	67	30	37	6.2	5.3	7.5	3.5	2.8	4.9
16	123	61	62	89	43	46	34	18	16	4.6	3.7	5.8	2.6	1.9	3.8
17	-	-	-	-	-	-	-	-	-	-	-	-	-	-	-
18	-	-	-	-	-	-	-	-	-	-	-	-	-	-	-
19	-	-	-	-	-	-	-	-	-	-	-	-	-	-	-
20	-	-	-	-	-	-	-	-	-	-	-	-	-	-	-
21	832	705	127	294	241	53	538	464	74	30.8	43.3	11.9	17.4	22.5	7.7
22	-	-	-	-	-	-	-	-	-	-	-	-	-	-	-
المجموع Total	4 784	3 137	1 647	2 434	1 430	1 004	2 350	1 707	643	177.2	192.6	153.7	100.0	100.0	100.0

(1) Causes of death given in annex 1

Calculations are made on the basis of population estimates taken from the United Nations
World Population Prospects: the 2008 Revision

(1) أسباب الوفيات في الملحق رقم 1
احتسبت المعدلات استنادا إلى تقديرات السكان الواردة في منشور الأمم المتحدة
"التوقعات السكانية في العالم، تنقيح عام 2008"

جدول 64 (تابع): أسباب الوفيات المسجلة : المعدل الخام والنسبة في المئة

Table 64 (cont'd): Registered Deaths by Cause: Crude Rates and Per Cent

KUWAIT 2000 — الكويت

سبب الوفاة (1) cause of death (1)	المجموع العام Grand Total			المواطنون Nationals			غير مواطنين Non-Nationals			المعدل الخام (لكل مائة ألف من السكان) Rate (per 100 thousand population)			النسبة في المئة percent		
	مجموع Total	رجال Men	نساء Women	مجموع Total	رجال Men	نساء Women	مجموع Total	رجال Men	نساء Women	مجموع Total	رجال Men	نساء Women	مجموع Total	رجال Men	نساء Women
1	98	63	35	51	32	19	47	31	16	4.4	4.6	4.0	2.3	2.3	2.3
2	519	269	250	323	166	157	196	103	93	23.3	19.9	28.6	12.3	10.0	6.3
3	243	132	111	187	102	85	56	30	26	10.9	9.7	12.7	5.7	4.9	7.2
4	20	14	6	16	12	4	4	2	2	0.9	1.0	0.7	0.5	0.5	0.4
5	11	9	2	8	6	2	3	3	-	0.5	0.7	0.2	0.3	0.3	0.1
6	73	49	24	39	27	12	34	22	12	3.3	3.6	2.7	1.7	1.8	1.6
7	1 695	1 133	562	914	541	373	781	592	189	76.1	83.6	64.3	40.1	42.1	36.6
8	203	104	99	132	70	62	71	34	37	9.1	7.7	11.3	4.8	3.9	6.4
9	103	69	34	59	38	21	44	31	13	4.6	5.1	3.9	2.4	2.6	2.2
10	86	49	37	66	38	28	20	11	9	3.9	3.6	4.2	2.0	1.8	2.4
11	4	-	4	-	-	-	4	-	4	0.2	-	0.5	0.1	-	0.3
12	4	1	3	3	1	2	1	-	1	0.2	0.1	0.3	0.1	0.0	0.2
13	1	1	-	1	1	-	-	-	-	0.0	0.1	-	0.0	0.0	-
14	201	108	93	126	68	58	75	40	35	9.0	8.0	10.6	4.8	4.0	6.1
15	160	99	61	98	59	39	62	40	22	7.2	7.3	7.0	3.8	3.7	4.0
16	147	69	78	103	53	50	44	16	28	6.6	5.1	8.9	3.5	2.6	5.1
17	659	521	138	294	234	60	365	287	78	29.6	38.5	15.8	15.6	19.4	9.0
18	-	-	-	-	-	-	-	-	-	-	-	-	-	-	-
المجموع Total	4 227	2 690	1 537	2 420	1 448	972	1 807	1 242	565	189.7	198.5	176.0	100.0	100.0	100.0

(1) Causes of death given in annex 1

Calculations are made on the basis of population estimates taken from the United Nations
World Population Prospects: the 2008 Revision

(1) أسباب الوفيات المدرجة في الملحق رقم 1

الحسابات مبنية على تقديرات السكان الواردة في منشور الأمم المتحدة
"التوقعات السكانية في العالم: تنقيح عام 2008"

-84-

جدول 64 (تابع) : أسباب الوفيات المسجلة : المعدل الخام والنسبة في المئة

Table 64 (cont'd): Registered Deaths by Cause: Crude Rates and Per Cent

OMAN عمان

2008

سبب الوفاة (1) cause of death (1)	المجموع العام Grand Total			المواطنون Nationals			غير مواطنين Non-Nationals			المعدل الخام (لكل مئة الف من السكان) Rate (per 100 thousand population)			النسبة في المئة percent		
	مجموع Total	رجال Men	نساء Women	مجموع Total	رجال Men	نساء Women	مجموع Total	رجال Men	نساء Women	مجموع Total	رجال Men	نساء Women	مجموع Total	رجال Men	نساء Women
1	335	223	112	23	17	6	312	206	106	12.0	14.2	9.2	4.5	4.7	4.2
2	403	245	158	22	15	7	381	230	151	14.5	15.6	13.0	5.4	5.2	5.9
3	284	165	119	15	13	2	269	152	117	10.2	10.5	9.8	3.8	3.5	4.5
4	53	34	19	-	-	-	53	34	19	1.9	2.2	1.6	0.7	0.7	0.7
5	10	6	4	-	-	-	10	6	4	0.4	0.4	0.3	0.1	0.1	0.1
6	65	49	16	10	7	3	55	42	13	2.3	3.1	1.3	0.9	1.0	0.6
7	1 395	845	550	129	108	21	1 266	737	529	50.1	53.7	45.4	18.8	17.8	20.6
8	407	256	151	24	16	8	383	240	143	14.6	16.3	12.5	5.5	5.4	5.7
9	147	113	34	21	19	2	126	94	32	5.3	7.2	2.8	2.0	2.4	1.3
10	156	102	54	2	1	1	154	101	53	5.6	6.5	4.5	2.1	2.1	2.0
11	4	-	4	-	-	-	4	-	4	0.1	-	0.3	0.1	-	0.1
12	39	22	17	1	-	1	38	22	16	1.4	1.4	1.4	0.5	0.5	0.6
13	8	3	5	2	1	1	6	2	4	0.3	0.2	0.4	0.1	0.1	0.2
14	125	71	54	10	6	4	115	65	50	4.5	4.5	4.5	1.7	1.5	2.0
15	130	75	55	8	5	3	122	70	52	4.7	4.8	4.5	1.8	1.6	2.1
16	3 152	1 948	1 204	553	440	113	2 599	1 508	1 091	113.2	123.8	99.3	42.5	41.0	45.1
17	-	-	-	-	-	-	-	-	-	-	-	-	-	-	-
18	-	-	-	-	-	-	-	-	-	-	-	-	-	-	-
19	-	-	-	-	-	-	-	-	-	-	-	-	-	-	-
20	-	-	-	-	-	-	-	-	-	-	-	-	-	-	-
21	702	591	111	197	173	24	505	418	87	25.2	37.6	9.2	9.5	12.4	4.2
22	-	-	-	-	-	-	-	-	-	-	-	-	-	-	-
المجموع Total	7 415	4 748	2 667	1 017	821	196	6 398	3 927	2 471	266.2	301.8	220.1	100.0	100.0	100.0

(1) Causes of death given in annex 1
Calculations are made on the basis of population estimates taken from the United Nations
World Population Prospects: the 2008 Revision

(1) أسباب الوفيات في الملحق رقم 1
احتسبت أسباب الوفيات استنادا إلى تقديرات السكان الواردة في منشور الأمم المتحدة
"توقعات السكانية في العالم: تنقيح عام 2008"

-85-

جدول 64 (تابع): أسباب الوفيات المسجلة: المعدل الخام والنسبة في السنة
Table 64 (cont'd): Registered Deaths by Cause: Crude Rates and Per Cent

عُمان (2) / OMAN (2)
2005

cause of death (1) سبب الوفاة (1)	Grand Total المجموع العام			Nationals المواطنين			Non-Nationals غير مواطنين			Rate (per 100 thousand population) المعدل الخام (لكل مائة ألف من السكان)			percent النسبة في السنة		
	Total مجموع	Men رجال	Women نساء	Total مجموع	Men رجال	Women نساء	Total مجموع	Men رجال	Women نساء	Total مجموع	Men رجال	Women نساء	Total مجموع	Men رجال	Women نساء
1	521	301	220	…	…	…	…	…	…	19.9	20.2	19.5	18.3	18.1	18.5
2	269	159	110	…	…	…	…	…	…	10.3	10.7	9.7	9.4	9.6	9.3
3	79	44	35	…	…	…	…	…	…	3.0	3.0	3.1	2.8	2.6	3.0
4	27	20	7	…	…	…	…	…	…	1.0	1.3	0.6	0.9	1.2	0.6
5	4	3	1	…	…	…	…	…	…	0.2	0.2	0.1	0.1	0.2	0.1
6	72	46	26	…	…	…	…	…	…	2.8	3.1	2.3	2.5	2.8	2.2
7	876	491	385	…	…	…	…	…	…	33.5	33.0	34.0	30.7	29.5	32.5
8	205	110	95	…	…	…	…	…	…	7.8	7.4	8.4	7.2	6.6	8.0
9	124	80	44	…	…	…	…	…	…	4.7	5.4	3.9	4.4	4.8	3.7
10	55	36	19	…	…	…	…	…	…	2.1	2.4	1.7	1.9	2.2	1.6
11	6	-	6	…	…	…	…	…	…	0.2	-	0.5	0.2	-	0.5
12	11	7	4	…	…	…	…	…	…	0.4	0.5	0.4	0.4	0.4	0.3
13	3	1	2	…	…	…	…	…	…	0.1	0.1	0.2	0.1	0.1	0.2
14	102	51	51	…	…	…	…	…	…	3.9	3.4	4.5	3.6	3.1	4.3
15	150	86	64	…	…	…	…	…	…	5.7	5.8	5.7	5.3	5.2	5.4
16	129	68	61	…	…	…	…	…	…	4.9	4.6	5.4	4.5	4.1	5.1
17	212	158	54	…	…	…	…	…	…	8.1	10.6	4.8	7.4	9.5	4.6
18	-	-	-	…	…	…	…	…	…	-	-	-	-	-	-
19	-	-	-	…	…	…	…	…	…	-	-	-	-	-	-
20	-	-	-	…	…	…	…	…	…	-	-	-	-	-	-
21	-	-	-	…	…	…	…	…	…	-	-	-	-	-	-
22	4	2	2	…	…	…	…	…	…	0.2	0.1	0.2	0.1	0.1	0.2
المجموع Total	2 849	1 663	1 186	…	…	…	…	…	…	108.8	111.8	104.9	100.0	100.0	100.0

(1) Causes of death given in annex 1
(2) Causes of deaths are for the deads in the hospital
Calculations are mades on the basis of population estimates taken from the United Nations
World Population Prospects: the 2008 Revision

(1) أسباب الوفيات في الملحق رقم 1
(2) الوفيات حسب السبب للمتوفين في المستشفيات
احتسبت المعدلات استنادا إلى تقديرات السكان الواردة في منشور الأمم المتحدة
"التوقعات للسكان في العالم، تنقيح عام 2008"

جدول 64 (تابع) : أسباب الوفيات المسجلة : المعدل الخام والنسبة في المئة

Table 64 (cont'd): Registered Deaths by Cause: Crude Rates and Per Cent

عمان (2) OMAN (2) — 2000

سبب الوفاة (1) cause of death (1)	المجموع العام Grand Total			المواطنون Nationals			غير مواطنين Non-Nationals			المعدل الخام (لكل مائة ألف من السكان) Rate (per 100 thousand population)			النسبة في المئة percent		
	مجموع Total	رجال Men	نساء Women	مجموع Total	رجال Men	نساء Women	مجموع Total	رجال Men	نساء Women	مجموع Total	رجال Men	نساء Women	مجموع Total	رجال Men	نساء Women
1	234	...	...	...	...	...	...	...	...	9.7	...	...	9.2	...	...
2	317	...	...	...	...	...	...	...	...	13.2	...	...	12.4	...	...
3	38	...	...	...	...	...	...	...	...	1.6	...	...	1.5	...	...
4	12	...	...	...	...	...	...	...	...	0.5	...	...	0.5	...	...
5	3	...	...	...	...	...	...	...	...	0.1	...	...	0.1	...	...
6	46	...	...	...	...	...	...	...	...	1.9	...	...	1.8	...	...
7	885	...	...	...	...	...	...	...	...	36.8	...	...	34.7	...	...
8	191	...	...	...	...	...	...	...	...	8.0	...	...	7.5	...	...
9	98	...	...	...	...	...	...	...	...	4.1	...	...	3.8	...	...
10	53	...	...	...	...	...	...	...	...	2.2	...	...	2.1	...	...
11	2	...	...	...	...	...	...	...	...	0.1	...	...	0.1	...	...
12	6	...	...	...	...	...	...	...	...	0.2	...	...	0.2	...	...
13	10	...	...	...	...	...	...	...	...	0.4	...	...	0.4	...	...
14	132	...	...	...	...	...	...	...	...	5.5	...	...	5.2	...	...
15	195	...	...	...	...	...	...	...	...	8.1	...	...	7.7	...	...
16	116	...	...	...	...	...	...	...	...	4.8	...	...	4.6	...	...
17	208	...	...	...	...	...	...	...	...	8.7	...	...	8.2	...	...
18	1	...	...	...	...	...	...	...	...	0.0	...	...	0.0	...	...
المجموع Total	2 547	1 593	1 008	...	...	...	...	...	...	106.0	114.5	99.8	100.0	100.0	100.0

(1) Causes of death given in annex 1
(2) Causes of deaths are for the deads in the hospital
Calculations are made on the basis of population estimates taken from the United Nations
World Population Prospects: the 2008 Revision

(1) أسباب الوفيات في الملحق رقم 1
(2) الوفيات حسب السبب للمتوفين في المستشفيات
احتسبت المعدلات استنادا إلى تقديرات السكان الواردة في منشور الأمم المتحدة
"التوقعات السكانية في العالم: تنقيح عام 2008"

جدول 64 (تابع) : أسباب الوفيات المسجلة : المعدل الخام والنسبة في المئة

Table 64 (cont'd): Registered Deaths by Cause: Crude Rates and Per Cent

PALESTINE 2007 — قلسطين

cause of death (1)	Grand Total المجموع العام			Nationals المواطنون			Non-Nationals غير مواطنين			Rate (per 100 thousand population) المعدل الخام (لكل مائة ألف من السكان)			percent النسبة في المئة		
سبب الوفاة (1)	Total	Men	Women	Total	Men	Women	Total	Men	Women	Total	Men	Women	Total	Men	Women
	مجموع	رجال	نساء	مجموع	رجال	نساء	مجموع	رجال	نساء	مجموع	رجال	نساء	مجموع	رجال	نساء
1	333	160	173	333	160	173	…	…	…	8.3	7.8	8.8	4.8	4.2	5.4
2	1 070	592	478	1 070	592	478	…	…	…	26.6	29.0	24.2	15.3	15.5	15.1
3	431	198	233	431	198	233	…	…	…	10.7	9.7	11.8	6.2	5.2	7.3
4	-	-	-	-	-	-	…	…	…	-	-	-	-	-	-
5							…	…	…						
6	108	54	54	108	54	54	…	…	…	2.7	2.6	2.7	1.5	1.4	1.7
7	2 737	1 503	1 234	2 737	1 503	1 234	…	…	…	68.1	73.5	62.5	39.1	39.3	38.9
8	628	356	272	628	356	272	…	…	…	15.6	17.4	13.8	9.0	9.3	8.6
9	118	69	49	118	69	49	…	…	…	2.9	3.4	2.5	1.7	1.8	1.5
10	393	215	178	393	215	178	…	…	…	9.8	10.5	9.0	5.6	5.6	5.6
11	1	-	1	1	-	1	…	…	…	0.0	-	0.1	0.0	-	0.0
12	-	-	-	-	-	-	…	…	…	-	-	-	-	-	-
13	-	-	-	-	-	-	…	…	…	-	-	-	-	-	-
14	292	167	125	292	167	125	…	…	…	7.3	8.2	6.3	4.2	4.4	3.9
15	807	466	341	807	466	341	…	…	…	20.1	22.8	17.3	11.5	12.2	10.7
16	81	44	37	81	44	37	…	…	…	2.0	2.2	1.9	1.2	1.2	1.2
17	-	-	-	-	-	-	…	…	…	-	-	-	-	-	-
18	-	-	-	-	-	-	…	…	…	-	-	-	-	-	-
19	-	-	-	-	-	-	…	…	…	-	-	-	-	-	-
20	-	-	-	-	-	-	…	…	…	-	-	-	-	-	-
21	-	-	-	-	-	-	…	…	…	-	-	-	-	-	-
22	-	-	-	-	-	-	…	…	…	-	-	-	-	-	-
Total المجموع	6 999	3 824	3 175	6 999	3 824	3 175	…	…	…	174	187	161	100	100	100

(1) Causes of death given in annex 1
Calculations are mades on the basis of population estimates taken from the United Nations World Population Prospects: the 2008 Revision

(1) أسباب الوفيات في الملحق رقم 1
الحسابات المجدولة استنادا إلى تقديرات السكان الواردة في منشور الأمم المتحدة "التوقعات السكانية في العالم: تنقيح عام 2008"

جدول 64 (تابع): أسباب الوفيات المسجلة : المعدل الخام والنسبة في المئة

Table 64 (cont'd): Registered Deaths by Cause: Crude Rates and Per Cent

فلسطين (2) PALESTINE[2]
2005

cause of death [1] سبب الوفاة [1]	المجموع العام Grand Total			المواطنون Nationals			غير مواطنين Non-Nationals			المعدل الخام (لكل مائة ألف من السكان) Rate (per 100 thousand population)			النسبة في المئة percent		
	مجموع Total	رجال Men	نساء Women	مجموع Total	رجال Men	نساء Women	مجموع Total	رجال Men	نساء Women	مجموع Total	رجال Men	نساء Women	مجموع Total	رجال Men	نساء Women
1	378	195	183	...	...	...	...	...	...	10.0	10.2	9.9	3.7	3.5	4.0
2	1 042	589	453	...	...	...	...	...	...	27.7	30.8	24.5	10.3	10.6	9.9
3	405	189	216	...	...	...	...	...	...	10.8	9.9	11.7	4.0	3.4	4.7
4	...	...	...	...	...	...	...	...	...	...	...	...	...	...	...
5															
6	128	66	62	...	...	...	...	...	...	3.4	3.4	3.4	1.3	1.2	1.4
7	3 773	1 943	1 830	...	...	...	...	...	...	100.3	101.6	99.0	37.2	34.9	40.1
8	696	380	316	...	...	...	...	...	...	18.5	19.9	17.1	6.9	6.8	6.9
9	103	60	43	...	...	...	...	...	...	2.7	3.1	2.3	1.0	1.1	0.9
10	405	208	197	...	...	...	...	...	...	10.8	10.9	10.7	4.0	3.7	4.3
11	1	-	1	...	...	...	...	...	...	0.0	-	0.1	0.0	-	0.0
12	...	...	...	...	...	...	...	...	...	...	...	...	...	...	...
13										...	...	...	...	...	...
14	504	257	247	...	...	...	...	...	...	13.4	13.4	13.4	5.0	4.6	5.4
15	874	490	384	...	...	...	...	...	...	23.2	25.6	20.8	8.6	8.8	8.4
16	573	283	290	...	...	...	...	...	...	15.2	14.8	15.7	5.7	5.1	6.3
17	...	...	...	...	...	...	...	...	...	...	...	...	...	...	...
18	...	...	...	...	...	...	...	...	...	...	...	...	...	...	...
19	...	...	...	...	...	...	...	...	...	...	...	...	...	...	...
20	...	...	...	...	...	...	...	...	...	...	...	...	...	...	...
21	547	447	100	...	...	...	...	...	...	14.5	23.4	5.4	5.4	8.0	2.2
22	707	462	245	...	...	...	...	...	...	18.8	24.1	13.3	5.4	8.3	5.4
المجموع Total	10 136	5 569	4 567	...	...	...	...	...	...	269.4	291.1	247.0	100.0	100.0	100.0

(1) Causes of death given in annex 1
(2) The source for the causes of deaths in this table is Population register
Calculations are made on the basis of population estimates taken from the United Nations
World Population Prospects: the 2008 Revision

(1) أسباب الوفيات في الملحق رقم 1
(2) مصدر أسباب الوفيات في هذا الجدول من تسجيل السكان
احتسبت المعدلات استنادا إلى تقديرات السكان الواردة في منشور الأمم المتحدة
"التوقعات السكانية في العالم: تنقيح عام 2008"

جدول 64 (تابع) : أسباب الوفيات المسجلة : المعدل الخام والنسبة في المئة

Table 64 (cont'd): Registered Deaths by Cause: Crude Rates and Per Cent

PALESTINE فلسطين 2000	المجموع العام Grand Total			المواطنين Nationals			غير مواطنين Non-Nationals			المعدل الخام (لكل مائة ألف من السكان) Rate (per 100 thousand population)			النسبة في المئة percent		
سبب الوفاة (1) cause of death (1)	مجموع Total	رجال Men	نساء Women	مجموع Total	رجال Men	نساء Women	مجموع Total	رجال Men	نساء Women	مجموع Total	رجال Men	نساء Women	مجموع Total	رجال Men	نساء Women
1	219	125	94	...	...	...	...	...	...	7.0	7.8	6.1	2.4	2.5	2.2
2	848	467	381	...	...	...	...	...	...	26.9	29.2	24.6	9.3	9.5	9.1
3	396	191	205	...	...	...	...	...	...	12.6	11.9	13.2	4.3	3.9	4.9
4	...	...	...	...	...	...	...	...	...	...	...	...	...	...	...
5	...	...	...	...	...	...	...	...	...	...	...	...	...	...	...
6	105	59	46	...	...	...	...	...	...	3.3	3.7	3.0	1.2	1.2	1.1
7 [2]	3 508	1 806	1 702	...	...	...	...	...	...	111.4	112.9	109.8	38.5	36.7	40.5
8	409	224	185	...	...	...	...	...	...	13.0	14.0	11.9	4.5	4.6	4.4
9	...	...	...	...	...	...	...	...	...	...	...	...	...	...	...
10 [3]	277	127	150	...	...	...	...	...	...	8.8	7.9	9.7	3.0	2.6	3.6
11	2 091	1 104	987	...	...	...	...	...	...	66.4	69.0	63.7	22.9	22.5	23.5
12	...	...	...	...	...	...	...	...	...	...	...	...	...	...	...
13	...	...	...	...	...	...	...	...	...	...	...	...	...	...	...
14	281	148	133	...	...	...	...	...	...	8.9	9.2	8.6	3.1	3.0	3.2
15	513	287	226	...	...	...	...	...	...	16.3	17.9	14.6	5.6	5.8	5.4
16	...	...	...	...	...	...	...	...	...	...	...	...	...	...	...
17	471	379	92	...	...	...	...	...	...	15.0	23.7	5.9	5.2	7.7	2.2
18 [4]															
المجموع Total	9 118	4 917	4 201	...	...	...	...	...	...	289.5	307.3	271.1	100.0	100.0	100.0

(1) Causes of death given in annex 1
(2) includes heart disease and hypertension
(3)includes kidney failure only

Calculations are made on the basis of population estimates taken from the United Nations World Population Prospects: the 2008 Revision

(1) أسباب الوفيات في الملحق رقم 1
(2) تشمل أمراض القلب وضغط الدم
(3) تشمل فشل الكلى الكلوي فقط

حسبت المعدلات استنادا إلى تقديرات السكان الواردة في منشور الأمم المتحدة "التوقعات السكانية في العالم: تنقيح عام 2008"

Table 64 (cont'd): Registered Deaths by Cause: Crude Rates and Per Cent

QATAR قطر

2008

النسبة في المئة — percent | المعدل الخام (لكل مئة ألف من السكان) Rate (per 100 thousand population) | غير مواطنين Non-Nationals | المواطنين Nationals | المجموع العام Grand Total

سبب الوفاة (1) cause of death (1)	مجموع Total	رجال Men	نساء Women	مجموع Total	رجال Men	نساء Women	مجموع Total	رجال Men	نساء Women	مجموع Total	رجال Men	نساء Women	مجموع Total	رجال Men	نساء Women
1	31	24	7	14	10	4	17	14	3	2.4	2.5	2.2	1.6	1.6	1.4
2	175	96	79	81	40	41	94	56	38	13.7	10.0	24.9	9.0	6.6	16.2
3	101	63	38	58	33	25	43	30	13	7.9	6.5	12.0	5.2	4.3	7.8
4	10	7	3	6	4	2	4	3	1	0.8	0.7	0.9	0.5	0.5	0.6
5	-	-	-	-	-	-	-	-	-	-	-	-	-	-	-
6	32	20	12	13	6	7	19	14	5	2.5	2.1	3.8	1.6	1.4	2.5
7	282	185	97	136	77	59	146	108	38	22.0	19.2	30.6	14.5	12.7	19.9
8	77	40	37	47	21	26	30	19	11	6.0	4.2	11.7	4.0	2.7	7.6
9	47	33	14	21	14	7	26	19	7	3.7	3.4	4.4	2.4	2.3	2.9
10	48	31	17	29	16	13	19	15	4	3.7	3.2	5.4	2.5	2.1	3.5
11	2	-	2	1	-	1	1	-	1	0.2	-	0.6	0.1	-	0.4
12	7	3	4	5	3	2	2	-	2	0.5	0.3	1.3	0.4	0.2	0.8
13	-	-	-	-	-	-	-	-	-	-	-	-	-	-	-
14	60	31	29	16	9	7	44	22	22	4.7	3.2	9.1	3.1	2.1	6.0
15	54	29	25	22	14	8	32	15	17	4.2	3.0	7.9	2.8	2.0	5.1
16	582	497	85	114	66	48	468	431	37	45.4	51.6	26.8	30.0	34.2	17.5
17	-	-	-	-	-	-	-	-	-	-	-	-	-	-	-
18	-	-	-	-	-	-	-	-	-	-	-	-	-	-	-
19	-	-	-	-	-	-	-	-	-	-	-	-	-	-	-
20	-	-	-	-	-	-	-	-	-	-	-	-	-	-	-
21	434	396	38	90	73	17	344	323	21	33.9	41.1	12.0	22.3	27.2	7.8
22	-	-	-	-	-	-	-	-	-	-	-	-	-	-	-
المجموع Total	1 942	1 455	487	653	386	267	1 289	1 069	220	151.6	151.0	153.6	100.0	100.0	100.0

(1) Causes of death given in annex 1

Calculations are made on the basis of population estimates taken from the United Nations
World Population Prospects: the 2008 Revision

(1) أسباب الوفيات في الملحق رقم 1

الحسابات المعدلات استندا إلى تقديرات السكان الواردة في منشور الأمم المتحدة
"التوقعات السكانية في العالم: تنقيح عام 2008"

جدول 64 (تابع) : أسباب الوفيات المسجلة : المعدل الخام والنسبة في المئة
Table 64 (cont'd): Registered Deaths by Cause: Crude Rates and Per Cent

QATAR — قطر — 2005

cause of death [1] سبب الوفاة [1]	Grand Total المجموع العام Total	Men رجال	Women نساء	Nationals المواطنين Total	Men رجال	Women نساء	Non-Nationals غير مواطنين Total	Men رجال	Women نساء	Rate (per 100 thousand population) المعدل الخام Total	Men رجال	Women نساء	percent النسبة في المئة Total	Men رجال	Women نساء
1	12	7	5	1	-	1	11	7	4	1.4	1.1	2.1	0.8	0.6	1.1
2	162	102	60	81	51	30	81	51	30	18.3	15.7	25.2	10.5	9.2	13.7
3	109	56	53	69	35	34	40	21	19	12.3	8.6	22.3	7.1	5.1	12.1
4	11	7	4	7	3	4	4	4	-	1.2	1.1	1.7	0.7	0.6	0.9
5	-	-	-	-	-	-	-	-	-	-	-	-	-	-	-
6	15	9	6	8	5	3	7	4	3	1.7	1.4	2.5	1.0	0.8	1.4
7	314	203	111	184	108	76	130	95	35	35.5	31.3	46.7	20.3	18.3	25.4
8	61	32	29	36	16	20	25	16	9	6.9	4.9	12.2	3.9	2.9	6.6
9	36	29	7	16	11	5	20	18	2	4.1	4.5	2.9	2.3	2.6	1.6
10	44	26	18	21	10	11	23	16	7	5.0	4.0	7.6	2.8	2.3	4.1
11	3	-	3	1	-	1	2	-	2	0.3	-	1.3	0.2	-	0.7
12	13	8	5	9	5	4	4	3	1	1.5	1.2	2.1	0.8	0.7	1.1
13	-	-	-	-	-	-	-	-	-	-	-	-	-	-	-
14	39	19	20	20	9	11	19	10	9	4.4	2.9	8.4	2.5	1.7	4.6
15	48	27	21	22	13	9	26	14	12	5.4	4.2	8.8	3.1	2.4	4.8
16	340	286	54	96	64	32	244	222	22	38.4	44.1	22.7	22.0	25.8	12.4
17	-	-	-	-	-	-	-	-	-	-	-	-	-	-	-
18	338	297	41	111	90	21	227	207	20	38.2	45.8	17.3	21.9	26.8	9.4
المجموع Total	1 545	1 108	437	682	420	262	863	688	175	174.5	171.0	183.9	100.0	100.0	100.0

(1) Causes of death given in annex 1

Calculations are made on the basis of population estimates taken from the United Nations
World Population Prospects: the 2008 Revision

(1) أسباب الوفاة في الملحق رقم 1

الحسابات تستند إلى تقديرات السكان الواردة في منشور الأمم المتحدة
"التوقعات السكانية في العالم، تنقيح عام 2008"

جدول 64 (تابع) : أسباب الوفيات المسجلة : المعدل الخام والنسبة في المئة

Table 64 (cont'd): Registered Deaths by Cause: Crude Rates and Per Cent

QATAR قطر

2000

سبب الوفاة (1) cause of death (1)	المجموع العام Grand Total			المواطنين Nationals			غير مواطنين Non-Nationals			المعدل الخام (لكل مئة ألف من السكان) Rate (per 100 thousand population)			النسبة في الألف Ratio (per %o)		
	مجموع Total	رجال Men	نساء Women	مجموع Total	رجال Men	نساء Women	مجموع Total	رجال Men	نساء Women	مجموع Total	رجال Men	نساء Women	مجموع Total	رجال Men	نساء Women
1	47	35	12	30	20	10	17	15	2	7.6	8.7	5.5	4.0	4.5	3.0
2	129	63	66	85	40	45	44	23	21	20.9	15.7	30.5	11.0	8.1	16.8
3	75	43	32	56	32	24	19	11	8	12.2	10.7	14.8	6.4	5.5	8.1
4	8	4	4	3	1	2	5	3	2	1.3	1.0	1.8	0.7	0.5	1.0
5	5	2	3	4	1	3	1	1	-	0.8	0.5	1.4	0.4	0.3	0.8
6	20	7	13	8	2	6	12	5	7	3.2	1.7	6.0	1.7	0.9	3.3
7	350	250	100	175	103	72	175	147	28	56.7	62.4	46.2	29.8	32.1	25.4
8	51	31	20	36	20	16	15	11	4	8.3	7.7	9.2	4.3	4.0	5.1
9	30	17	13	14	5	9	16	12	4	4.9	4.2	6.0	2.6	2.2	3.3
10	65	40	25	43	23	20	22	17	5	10.5	10.0	11.6	5.5	5.1	6.3
11	-	-	-	-	-	-	-	-	-	-	-	-	-	-	-
12	-	-	-	-	-	-	-	-	-	-	-	-	-	-	-
13	5	1	4	1	-	1	4	1	3	0.8	0.2	1.8	0.4	0.1	1.0
14	57	22	35	29	10	19	28	12	16	9.2	5.5	16.2	4.9	2.8	8.9
15	52	34	18	25	17	8	27	17	10	8.4	8.5	8.3	4.4	4.4	4.6
16	103	76	27	34	20	14	69	56	13	16.7	19.0	12.5	8.8	9.8	6.9
17	176	154	22	71	58	13	105	96	9	28.5	38.5	10.2	15.0	19.8	5.6
18	-	-	-	-	-	-	-	-	-	-	-	-	-	-	-
المجموع Total	1 173	779	394	614	352	262	559	427	132	190.2	194.5	182.1	100.0	100.0	100.0

(1) Causes of death given in annex 1

Calculations are made on the basis of population estimates taken from the United Nations
World Population Prospects: the 2008 Revision

(1) أسباب الوفيات معطاة في الملحق رقم 1

احتسبت المعدلات استنادا إلى تقديرات السكان الواردة في منشور الأمم المتحدة
"التوقعات عام 2008"

-93-

جدول 64 (ثاني) : أسباب الوفيات المسجلة : المعدل الخام والنسبة في المئة

Table 64 (cont'd): Registered Deaths by Cause: Crude Rates and Per Cent

الإمارات العربية المتحدة **UNITED ARAB EMIRATES** 2000

سبب الوفاة (1) cause of death (1)	المجموع العام Grand Total			المواطنون Nationals			غير مواطنين Non-Nationals			المعدل الخام (لكل مائة ألف من السكان) Rate (per 100 thousand population)			النسبة في المئة Ratio (per %)		
	مجموع Total	رجال Men	نساء Women	مجموع Total	رجال Men	نساء Women	مجموع Total	رجال Men	نساء Women	مجموع Total	رجال Men	نساء Women	مجموع Total	رجال Men	نساء Women
1	41	25	16	15	10	5	26	15	11	1.3	1.1	1.5	0.8	0.6	1.1
2	468	268	200	194	106	88	274	162	112	14.5	12.3	19.0	8.7	6.8	13.5
3	158	86	72	94	46	48	64	40	24	4.9	3.9	6.8	2.9	2.2	4.9
4	121	71	50	74	37	37	47	34	13	3.7	3.2	4.8	2.2	1.8	3.4
5	4	3	1	1	1	-	3	2	1	0.1	0.1	0.1	0.1	0.1	0.1
6	33	15	18	18	8	10	15	7	8	1.0	0.7	1.7	0.6	0.4	1.2
7	1 383	1 000	383	560	311	249	823	689	134	42.7	45.8	36.4	25.6	25.5	25.9
8	189	119	70	114	67	47	75	52	23	5.8	5.4	6.7	3.5	3.0	4.7
9	111	85	26	41	26	15	70	59	11	3.4	3.9	2.5	2.1	2.2	1.8
10	152	89	63	87	50	37	65	39	26	4.7	4.1	6.0	2.8	2.3	4.3
11	1	-	1	-	-	-	1	-	1	0.0	-	0.1	0.0	-	0.1
12	-	-	-	-	-	-	-	-	-	-	-	-	-	-	-
13	-	-	-	-	-	-	-	-	-	-	-	-	-	-	-
14	260	146	114	118	66	52	142	80	62	8.0	6.7	10.8	4.8	3.7	7.7
15	133	76	57	62	36	26	71	40	31	4.1	3.5	5.4	2.5	1.9	3.9
16	981	713	268	414	255	159	567	458	109	30.3	32.6	25.5	18.2	18.2	18.1
17	809	709	100	232	192	40	577	517	60	25.0	32.4	9.5	15.0	18.1	6.8
18	552	511	41	134	115	19	418	396	22	17.0	23.4	3.9	10.2	13.0	2.8
المجموع Total	5 396	3 916	1 480	2 158	1 326	832	3 238	2 590	648	166.6	179.2	140.6	100.0	100.0	100.0

(1) Causes of death given in annex 1

Calculations are made on the basis of population estimates taken from the United Nations
World Population Prospects: the 2008 Revision

(1) أسباب الوفيات المدرجة في الملحق رقم 1
احتسبت المعدلات استناداً إلى تقديرات السكان الواردة في منشور الأمم المتحدة
"التوقعات السكانية في العالم: تنقيح عام 2008"

ملحق رقم 1: التصنيف الدولي لأسباب الوفاة
Annex 1: International Classification of Causes of Death

Serial no.	Cause of Death	سبب الوفاة	رقم مسلسل
1	Certain infectious and parasitic diseases	امراض معدية وطفيلية معينة	1
2	Neoplasms	الاورام	2
3	Endocrine, nutritional and metabolic dseases	امراض الغدد الصماء والتغذية والتمثيل الغذائي	3
4	Disorders of the blood and blood-forming organs and certain disorders involving the immune mechanism	اضطرابات الدم واعضاء تكوين الدم واضطرابات معينة تشمل اضطرابات المناعة	4
5	Mental and behavioural disorders	الاضطرابات العقلية والسلوكية	5
6	Diseases of the nervous system	امراض الجهاز العصبي واعضاء الحس	6
7	Diseases of the circulatory system	امراض الجهاز الدوري الدموي	7
8	Diseases of the respiratory system	امراض الجهاز التنفسي	8
9	Diseases of the digestive system	امراض الجهاز الهضمي	9
10	Diseases of the genitourinary system	امراض الجهاز التناسلي البولي	10
11	Pregnancy, child birth and the puerperium	مضاعفات الحمل والولادة والنفاس	11
12	Diseases of the skin and subcutaneous tissue	امراض الجلد والنسيج تحت الجلد	12
13	Diseases of the musculoskeletal system and connective tissue	امراض الجهاز الهيكلي العظمي والنسيج الضام	13
14	Congenital malformations, deformations and chromosomal abnormalities	تشوهات خلقية وعاهات وشذوذ كروموزي	14
15	Certain conditions originating in the perinental period	اسباب معينة لحالات المرضى والوفاة حول موعد الولادة	15
16	Symptoms, signs and abnormal clinical and laboratory findings, not elsewhere classified	امراض وحالات غير معينة وغير مشخصة في مكان اخر	16
17	Injury, poisoning and certain other consequences of external causes	الاصابات والتسمم ونتائج اخرى معينة لاسباب خارجية	17
18	Codes for special purposes	حالات غير مشخصة	18
19	Diseases of the eye and adnexa	امراض النظر	19
20	Diseases of the ear and mastoid process	امراض السمع	20
21	External causes of morbidity and mortality	لاسباب خارجية للمرضى والوفاة	21
22	Factors influencing health status and contact with health services	عوامل تؤثر على الوضيع الصحي واتصال بالخدمات الصحية	22

القسم الثالث
Section Three

الزواج والطلاق
Marriages and Divorces

يعرض القسم الثالث من هذه النشرة، المعنون "الزواج والطلاق"، بيانات عن متوسط العمر عند الزواج الأول، والمعدلات الخام للزواج والطلاق في منطقة الإسكوا للأعوام 1990 و1995 و2000 وحتى آخر سنة تتوافر فيها البيانات عن كل بلد[1]. ويحتوي هذا القسم على 5 جداول و13 شكل بياني.

شمل هذا القسم بيانات عن متوسط العمر عند الزواج الأول للنساء وللرجال بالإضافة إلى مجموع الزواج والطلاق الخاصة بها والتي تم احتسابها اعتماداً على تقديرات السكان المستمدة من آفاق سكان العالم (نشرة السكان بالأمم المتحد، إدارة الشؤون الاقتصادية والاجتماعية في الأمم المتحدة، 2008 عن شعبة السكان بالأمم المتحد، إدارة الشؤون الاقتصادية والاجتماعية.

Section III of this Bulletin, entitled "Marriage and Divorce", presents data on mean age at first marriage, crude rates of marriage and divorce in the ESCWA region for the years 1990, 1995 and from 2000 to the most recent year for which data is available for each country[1]. This section contains 5 tables and 13 charts.

Data on mean age at first marriage for women and men as well as number of marriages and divorces in the total population with their respective crude rates which have been calculated based on the population estimates from the United Nations Population Division, Department of Economic and Social Affairs (DESA), *World Population Prospects, revision 2008.*

[1] المعدلات المعروضة في هذا القسم محتسبة بناء على البيانات الوطنية عن الزواج والطلاق.

(1) The rates presented in this section have been calculated on the basis of national figures for the number of marriages and divorces.

جدول الزواج 65: في بلدان الإسكوا 1990-2008
Table 65: Marriages in ESCWA countries 1990-2008

	1990	1995	2000	2001	2002	2003	2004	2005	2006	2007	2008	
Bahrain	2 942	3 321	3 963	4 504	4 909	5 373	4 929	4 669	4 724	4 981	...	البحرين
Egypt	405 141	470 513	592 381	457 534	510 517	537 092	550 709	522 751	522 887	614 848	660 159	مصر
Iraq	143 518	120 692	171 134	...	...	256 494	262 554	...	...	...	...	العراق
Jordan	32 706	35 501	45 618	49 794	46 873	48 784	53 754	56 418	59 335	60 548	...	الأردن
Kuwait	...	9 515	...	...	...	...	...	12 419	12 584	13 315	...	الكويت
Lebanon	29 945	30 758	32 564	32 225	31 653	30 636	30 014	29 705	29 078	35 796	37 593	لبنان
Oman	...	...	...	...	...	...	...	...	...	...	...	عمان
Palestine	...	...	...	...	...	...	...	...	...	65 370	67 548	فلسطين
Qatar	1 370	1 488	2 096	2 194	2 351	2 550	2 649	2 734	3 019	3 206	3 235	قطر
Saudi Arabia	...	67934[1]	79 595	81 576	90 982	98 343	111 063	105 066	115 549	130 451	...	المملكة العربية السعودية
Sudan	...										...	السودان
Syrian Arab Republic										237 592		الجمهورية العربية السورية
United Arab Emirates	7 357	6 475	8 970	10 030	11 285	12 277	12 794	12 984	13 190	12 987	15 041	الإمارات العربية المتحدة
Yemen	...	11448[2]	5 375	9 120	10 934	600	715	...			...	اليمن
TOTAL	622 979	678 263	941 696	646 977	709 504	992 149	1029 181	746 746	760 366	1179 094	783 576	المجموع

جدول معدل الزواج 66: الخام لكل ألف من السكان في بلدان الإسكوا 1990-2008
Table 66: Crude Marriage Rate (per'000) population in ESCWA countries 1990-2008

	1990	1995	2000	2001	2002	2003	2004	2005	2006	2007	2008	
Bahrain	6.0	5.7	6.1	6.8	7.2	7.7	6.9	6.4	6.4	6.6	...	البحرين
Egypt	7.0	7.4	8.4	6.4	7.0	7.2	7.3	6.8	6.7	7.7	8.1	مصر
Iraq	7.9	5.8	6.9	...	...	9.5	9.5	...	...	...	...	العراق
Jordan	10.1	8.2	9.4	10.0	9.2	9.3	10.0	10.1	10.3	10.2	...	الأردن
Kuwait	...	5.5	...	...	...	...	...	4.6	4.5	4.7	...	الكويت
Lebanon	10.1	8.8	8.6	8.4	8.1	7.7	7.5	7.3	7.0	8.6	9.0	لبنان
Oman	...	...	...	...	...	...	...	...	...	...	...	عمان
Palestine	...	...	...	...	...	...	...	...	...	16.3	16.3	فلسطين
Qatar	2.9	2.8	3.4	3.4	3.4	3.5	3.3	3.1	3.0	2.8	2.5	قطر
Saudi Arabia	...	3.7	3.8	3.8	4.1	4.4	4.8	4.4	4.8	5.3	...	المملكة العربية السعودية
Sudan	...										...	السودان
Syrian Arab Republic										11.6		الجمهورية العربية السورية
United Arab Emirates	3.9	2.7	2.8	2.9	3.1	3.3	3.3	3.2	3.1	3.0	3.4	الإمارات العربية المتحدة
Yemen	0.0	0.7	0.3	0.5	0.6	...	...	...			...	اليمن

(1) 1993 data   بيانات 1993 (1)
(2) 1997 data   بيانات 1997 (2)

Calculations are mades on the basis of population estimates taken
from the United Nations World Population Prospects: the 2008

احتسبت المعدلات استنادا إلى تقديرات السكان الواردة في منشور الأمم المتحدة
"التوقعات السكانية في العالم: تنقيح عام 2008"

جدول 67: الطلاق في بلدان الإسكوا 1990-2008
Table 67: Divorces in ESCWA countries 1990-2008

	1990	1995	2000	2001	2002	2003	2004	2005	2006	2007	2008	
Bahrain	590	691	769	801	838	923	1 030	1 051	1 141	1 198	...	البحرين
Egypt	67 195	67 653	68 991	70 279	70 069	69 867	64 496	65 047	65 461	77 878	84 430	مصر
Iraq	...	33 161	...	...	...	...	...	...	...	...	...	العراق
Jordan	5 074	6 315	8 241	9 017	9 032	9 022	9 791	10 231	11 413	11 793	...	الأردن
Kuwait	...	3 015	3 649	3 851	3 891	3 998	4 899	4 538	4 239	4 945	...	الكويت
Lebanon	3 026	3 869	4 282	4 480	4 060	4 328	4 372	4 746	4 388	5 859	5 389	لبنان
Oman	...	...	...	...	...	26 359	...	...	...	...	...	عمان
Palestine	...	...	...	...	...	...	...	...	...	8 086	8 798	فلسطين
Qatar	359	474	615	566	732	790	787	643	826	997	939	قطر
Saudi Arabia	...	13227*	18 583	16 725	18 765	20 794	24 435	24 318	24 428	28 561	...	المملكة العربية السعودية
Sudan	...	...	...	...	...	...	...	...	...	...	...	السودان
Syrian Arab Republic	...	...	...	...	...	...	...	...	...	19 506	...	الجمهورية العربية السورية
United Arab Emirates	1 994	2 256	2 392	2 832	3 390	3 243	3 577	2 796	2 491	2 783	3 855	الإمارات العربية المتحدة
Yemen	...	2249**	507	617	998	104	33	...	...	...	...	اليمن
TOTAL	78 238	117 434	108 029	109 168	111 775	139 428	113 420	113 370	114 387	161 606	103 411	المجموع

جدول 68: معدل الطلاق الخام لكل ألف من السكان بلدان الإسكوا 1990-2008
Table 68: Crude Divorce Rate (per'000) population in ESCWA countries 1990-2008

	1990	1995	2000	2001	2002	2003	2004	2005	2006	2007	2008	
Bahrain	1.2	1.2	1.2	1.2	1.2	1.3	1.4	1.4	1.5	1.6	...	البحرين
Egypt	1.2	1.1	1.0	1.0	1.0	0.9	0.9	0.8	0.8	1.0	1.0	مصر
Iraq	...	1.6	...	...	...	...	...	...	...	...	...	العراق
Jordan	1.6	1.5	1.7	1.8	1.8	1.7	1.8	1.8	2.0	2.0	...	الأردن
Kuwait	...	1.7	1.6	1.6	1.6	1.6	1.9	1.7	1.5	1.7	...	الكويت
Lebanon	1.0	1.1	1.1	1.2	1.0	1.1	1.1	1.2	1.1	1.4	1.3	لبنان
Oman	...	...	...	...	...	10.4	...	...	...	...	...	عمان
Palestine	...	...	...	...	...	...	...	...	...	2.0	2.1	فلسطين
Qatar	0.8	0.9	1.0	0.9	1.1	1.1	1.0	0.7	0.8	0.9	0.7	قطر
Saudi Arabia	...	0.7	0.9	0.8	0.9	0.9	1.1	1.0	1.0	1.2	...	المملكة العربية السعودية
Sudan	...	...	...	...	...	...	...	...	...	...	...	السودان
Syrian Arab Republic	...	...	...	...	...	...	...	...	...	...	...	الجمهورية العربية السورية
United Arab Emirates	1.1	0.9	0.7	0.8	0.9	0.9	0.9	0.7	0.6	0.6	0.9	الإمارات العربية المتحدة
Yemen	...	0.1	0.0	0.0	0.1	0.0	0.0	...	...	...	...	اليمن

(1) 1993 data — بيانات 1993 (1)
(2) 1997 data — بيانات 1997 (2)

Calculations are made on the basis of population estimates taken from the United Nations World Population Prospects: the 2008 Revision

احتسبت المعدلات استنادا إلى تقديرات السكان الواردة في منشور الأمم المتحدة "توقعات السكان في العالم: تنقيح عام 2008"

2008-1990 معدل الزواج الخام ومعدل الطلاق الخام لكل ألف من السكان للبلدان الأعضاء حسب توفر البيانات

Marriage and Divorce Crude Rates (per '000) population for member countries according to data availability1990-2008

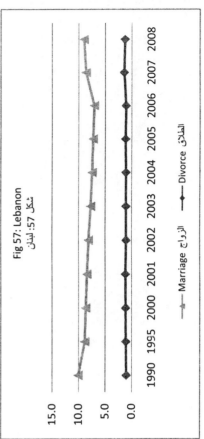

Fig 55: Egypt
شكل 55: مصر

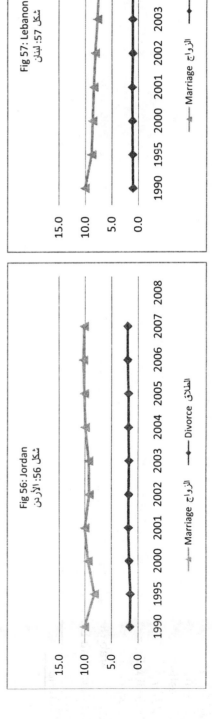

Fig 57: Lebanon
شكل 57: لبنان

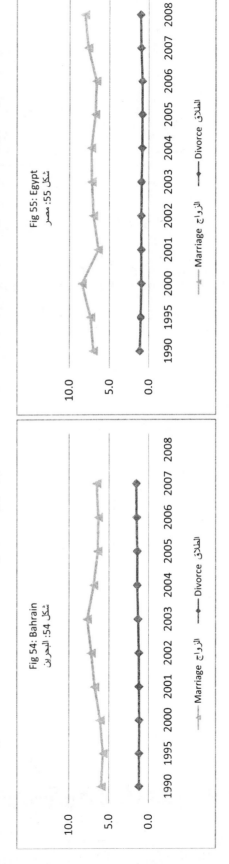

Fig 54: Bahrain
شكل 54: البحرين

Fig 56: Jordan
شكل 56: الأردن

معدل الزواج الخام ومعدل الطلاق الخام لكل ألف من السكان للبلدان الأعضاء حسب توفر البيانات 1990-2008 (تابع)

Marriage and Divorce Crude Rates (per '000) population for member countries according to data availability1990-2008 (cont'd)

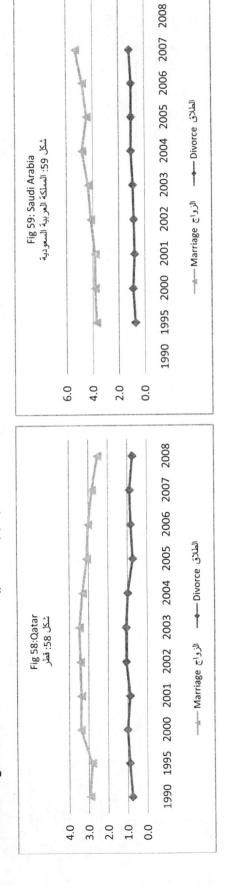

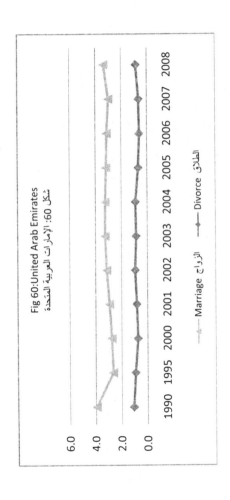

جدول 69: متوسط العمر عند الزواج الأول في بلدان الإسكوا

Table 69: Mean Age at First Marriage in the ESCWA countries

| | 1990 | | 1995 | | 2000 | | 2005 | | 2006 | | 2007 | | 2008 | |
| | رجال | نساء | رجال | نساء | رجال | نساء | رجال | نساء | رجال | نساء | رجال | نساء | رجال | نساء |
	Men	Women	Men	Women	Men	Women	Men	Women	Men	Women	Men	Women	Men	Women
Bahrain البحرين	26.1	22.3	26.3	22.2	26.3	25.0	26.5	22.7	27.6	23.2	26.86	25.42	...	23.2
Egypt مصر	28.7	22.1	29.0	26.7	28.6	25.3	28.8	23.2	28.8	23.0	28.5	23.5	28.2	23.2
Iraq العراق	...	...	...	...	...	...	...	...	...	...	...	...	...	...
Jordan الأردن	25.9	21.5	26.4	21.9	28.9	25.9	29.7	26.8	29.8	26.8	29.4	26.3	29.8	26.3
Kuwait الكويت	...	...	...	...	...	...	...	...	...	...	...	...	...	...
Lebanon لبنان	...	...	...	...	...	...	...	...	...	...	...	...	...	...
Oman عمان	...	...	...	...	...	...	...	...	...	...	...	...	...	...
Palestine فلسطين	...	...	...	...	...	...	...	...	...	...	...	...	...	...
Qatar قطر	...	...	26.3	23.0	27.5	24.0	27.4	24.3	27.3	24.3	27.5	24.6	...	...
Saudi Arabia المملكة العربية السعودية	...	...	...	...	...	...	...	...	...	...	...	...	...	...
Sudan السودان	...	...	...	...	...	...	...	...	...	...	...	...	...	...
Syrian Arab Republic الجمهورية العربية السورية	...	...	...	...	...	...	...	...	...	...	...	...	...	...
United Arab Emirates الإمارات العربية المتحدة	...	...	...	...	...	...	...	...	...	...	...	...	...	...
Yemen اليمن	...	...	...	...	...	...	...	...	...	...	...	...	...	...

متوسط العمر عند الزواج الأول للرجال و النساء للبلدان الأعضاء حسب توفر البيانات 2008-1990

2008-1990
Mean Age at First Marriage for Women and Men for member countries according to data availability 1990-2008

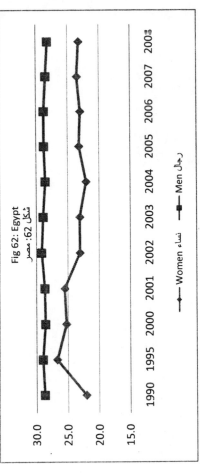

Fig 62: Egypt
شكل 62: مصر

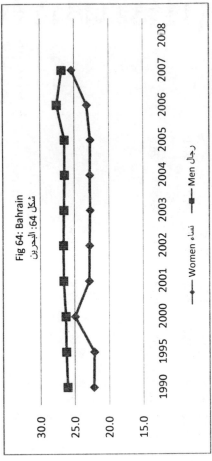

Fig 64: Bahrain
شكل 64: البحرين

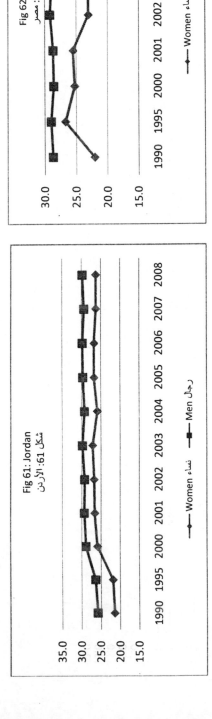

Fig 61: Jordan
شكل 61: الأردن

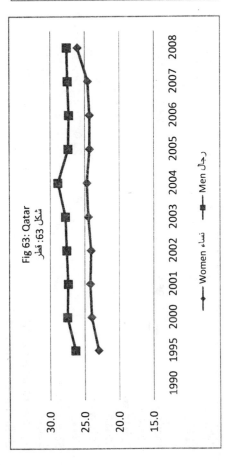

Fig 63: Qatar
شكل 63: قطر

متوسط العمر عند الزواج الأول في بلدان الإسكوا حسب توفر البيانات 1990-2008

Mean Age at First Marriage in ESCWA countries according to data availability 1990-2008

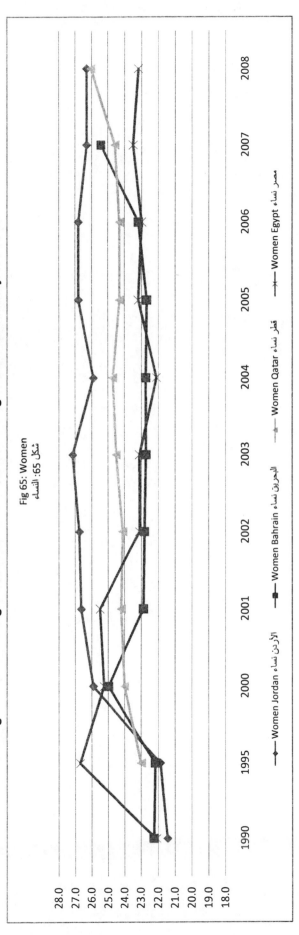

Fig 65: Women
شكل 65: النساء

— Women Jordan الأردن نساء — Women Bahrain البحرين نساء — Women Qatar قطر نساء — Women Egypt مصر نساء

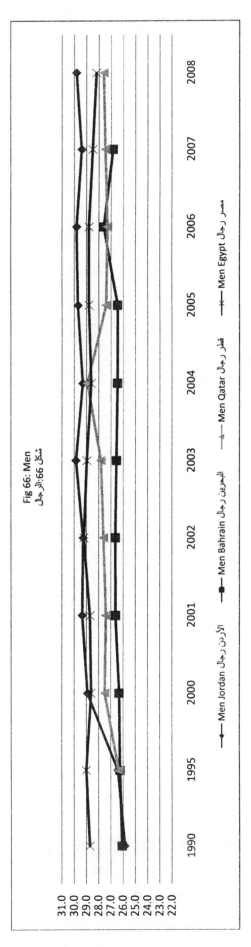

Fig 66: Men
شكل 66: الرجال

— Men Jordan الأردن رجال — Men Bahrain البحرين رجال — Men Qatar قطر رجال — Men Egypt مصر رجال

TECHNICAL NOTES

1. Crude birth rate (CBR)

The number of live births (B^t_o) occurring during a particular calendar year (or average annual births in a given period) in a particular area per 1,000 mid-year total population (P):

$$CBR = \frac{B^t_o}{P} \times 1000$$

2. Crude death rate (CDR)

The number of deaths in a particular area during a calendar year (or annual average deaths in a given period) (D^t_o) per 1,000 of mid-year total population (P):

$$CDR = \frac{D^t_o}{P} \times 1000$$

3. Rate of natural increase (r)

The difference between the number of live births and deaths occurring in a year, expressed as a percentage of the base population of that year. This measure of population change excludes the effects of migration expressed as a percentage of the base population of that year:

$$RNI = \frac{B^t_o - D^t_o}{P} \times 100$$

$$\text{or } RNI = \frac{CBR - CDR}{10}$$

4. Foetal death rate (FDR)

The number of foetal deaths occurring in the population of a

المنهجية

1- معدل المواليد الخام

وهو عدد المواليد الأحياء (B^t_o) خلال سنة معينة (أو المتوسط السنوي للولادات في فترة معينة) لكل ألف من مجموع السكان في منتصف السنة (P). ويحسب كالتالي:

2- معدل الوفيات الخام

وهو عدد الوفيات التي تحدث في مكان معين خلال سنة معينة (أو المتوسط السنوي للوفيات في فترة معينة) (D^t_o) لكل ألف من مجموع السكان في منتصف السنة (P). ويحسب كالتالي:

3- معدل الزيادة الطبيعية

وهو الفرق بين عدد المواليد الأحياء وعدد الوفيات التي تحصل في تلك السنة. وفي قياس تغير القاعدة السكانية بهذه الطريقة يستثنى تأثيرات الهجرة، محسوبا كنسبة مئوية من القاعدة السكانية في تلك السنة. ويحسب كالتالي:

4- معدل وفيات الأجنة

وهو عدد وفيات الأجنة التي تحدث بين سكان منطقة جغرافية معينة في

سنة معينة لكل ألف من مجموع الولادات (وتشمل هذه الولادات المواليد الأحياء والأجنة المتوفاة). ويحسب كالتالي:

$$FDR = \frac{foetal\ deaths}{live\ births + foetal\ deaths} \times 1000$$

given geographical area in a given year per 1,000 total births (live births plus foetal deaths):

5- معدل وفيات الرضّع

وهو عدد وفيات الرضّع (الذي لا يشمل وفيات الأجنة) التي تحدث في الفترة بين الولادة والسنة الأولى من العمر في سكان منطقة معينة خلال سنة معينة (أو المتوسط السنوي لوفيات الرضّع في فترة معينة) (D^t_0) لكل ألف من المواليد الأحياء (B^t). ويحسب كالتالي:

$$IMR = \frac{D^t_0}{B^t} \times 1000$$

5. Infant mortality rate (IMR)

The number of infant deaths (excluding foetal deaths) between birth and first birthday in the population of a given area during a calendar year (or annual average infant death rate in a given period) (D^t_0) per 1,000 live births (B^t):

6- معدل وفيات الأطفال

وهو أرجحية الوفاة قبل بلوغ سن الخامسة من المواليد الأحياء. ويقاس بعدد وفيات الأطفال لكل ألف من المواليد الأحياء. ويحسب كالتالي:

$$U5MR = \frac{child\ deaths}{live\ births} \times 1000$$

6. Child mortality rate (U5MR)

The probability of dying before the age of five, expressed as deaths under the age of five per 1,000 live births:

7- نسبة الوفيات النفاسية

وهي عدد الوفيات الناتجة عن أسباب نفاسية بين النساء من سكان منطقة جغرافية معينة في سنة معينة لكل مائة ألف من المواليد الأحياء في تلك المنطقة وتلك السنة. ويحسب كالتالي:

$$MMR = \frac{maternal\ deaths}{live\ births} \times 100,000$$

7. Maternal mortality ratio (MMR)

The number of deaths from puerperal causes in the female population of a given geographical area in a given year per 100,000 live births in that area in that year:

8- معدل الخصوبة العام

وهو عدد المواليد الأحياء في سنة معينة (أو متوسط عدد المواليد

8. General fertility rate (GFR)

The number of live births in a particular calendar year (or average live births in a given period) in a given area (B^t_0) per 1,000 mid-year female population of childbearing age (15-49) (F_{15-49}):

$$GFR = \frac{B^t_o}{F_{15-49}} \times 1000$$

9. Age-specific fertility rate (ASFR)

The number of births ($_nB_x$) per 1,000 women in a particular age group ($_nF_x$) during a calendar year:

$$ASFR = \frac{_nB_x}{_nF_x} \times 1000$$

10. Total fertility rate (TFR)

The number of children that would be born to a woman if she were to live to the end of her childbearing years (15-49) and if the likelihood of her giving birth to children at any given age were to be the currently-prevailing age-specific fertility rate. It is the total of all the age-specific fertility rates defined over a five-year interval (n):

$$TFR = n \sum_{15}^{49} \left(\frac{_nB_x}{_nF_x} \right)$$

11. Gross reproduction rate (GRR)

The GRR is based on ASFR and identical to TFR, but refers only to female births. It indicates how many daughters a woman would bear during her lifetime if, throughout her reproductive life, she were subject to the age-specific rate of bearing female children as recorded for a particular year or another given interval. A close approximation of GRR can be obtained by multiplying TFR by the proportion of female births to all births in a given period.

الأحياء في فترة معينة (B'ₒ) لكل ألف امرأة في سن الإنجاب (من عمر 15 سنة إلى 49 سنة) (F_{15-49}) من مجموع السكان في منتصف السنة. ويحسب كالتالي:

9- معدل الخصوبة العمرية

وهو عدد المواليد ($_nB_x$) لكل ألف امرأة من فئة عمرية معينة ($_nF_x$) خلال سنة معينة. ويحسب كالتالي:

10- معدل الخصوبة الكلي

وهو عدد الأطفال الذين من المفترض أن يولدوا لامرأة معينة إذا عاشت حتى نهاية فترتها الإنجابية (من عمر 15 إلى 49 سنة) وإذا كانت احتمالات أن تلد ولا في أي عمر معين تتم وفقاً لمعدل الخصوبة العمرية السائد خلال السنة المعينة. وبلغ احتساب معدل الخصوبة الكلية بجمع كل معدلات الخصوبة العمرية المحددة في فترات فاصلة من خمس سنوات (n)، وذلك وفق المعادلة التالية:

$$TFR = n \sum_{15}^{49} \left(\frac{_nB_x}{_nF_x} \right)$$

11- معدل الإحلال الإجمالي

وهو مبني على أساس معدل الخصوبة العمرية (ASFR) وشاظر تماماً لمعدل الخصوبة الكلية (TFR) غير أنه يعود إلى المواليد الإناث فقط. ويشير إلى عدد المواليد الإناث لامرأة ما خلال فترتها الإنجابية، إذا ما أطبق عليها معدل الخصوبة العمرية لإنجاب الإناث المسجل خلال سنة معينة أو لفترة زمنية فاصلة معينة. ويمكن الحصول على تقدير قريب جداً لمعدل الخصوبة الكلية (TFR) بنسبة المواليد الإناث من اجمالي المواليد في فترة معينة.

12. Mean age at childbearing

The mean age of women when their children are born. For a given calendar year, the mean age of women at childbearing is the weighted average of the different ages (the reproductive period is generally considered to be 15-49 years of age), using as weights the age-specific fertility rates (ASFR) (that is, the number of live births to mothers of age x to the average female population of age x). Depending on the country, the age is either the age reached during the year or the age at last birthday.

13. Crude death rate by cause (CDRc)

The number of deaths from a given cause or group of causes in a given area during a calendar year (or annual average across a given period) (D^t_c) per 100,000 of the mid-year total population (P):

$$CDRc = \frac{D^t_c}{P} \times 100{,}000$$

14. Mean age at first marriage

The mean age at which an individual first marries. For a given calendar year, it can be calculated using the first marriage rates by age (that is, the number of first marriages at age x in relation to the average population of age x). Using this calculation, the mean age is not weighted, meaning that the number of women or men at each age is not taken into account.

15. Crude marriage rate (CMR)

The ratio of the number of marriages in a given area during a calendar year (or annual average across a given period) (M^t_o) to the average population (P) in the same period and the same area per 1,000 inhabitants:

$$CMR = \frac{M^t_o}{P} \times 1000$$

12- متوسط عمر المرأة عند الإنجاب

يُعتبر متوسط عمر المرأة عند الإنجاب في سنة معينة المتوسط المرجّح لأعمار المختلفة (حيث تُعتبر الفترة الإنجابية عموما بين سن 15 و 49 سنة). ويُحتسب باستخدام معدلات الخصوبة العمرية كعامل مرجّح (أي عدد المواليد الأحياء لمجموع الإنجاب بسن (x) إلى متوسط عدد النساء بسن (x) من السكان). وتكون السن إما السن التي تم بلوغها خلال السنة المعينة أو السن في آخر عيد ميلاد).

13- معدل الوفيات الخام بحسب السبب

وهو عدد الوفيات الناتجة عن سبب معين أو مجموعة معينة من الأسباب في منطقة معينة خلال سنة معينة (أو المتوسط السنوي لفترة زمنية معينة)(D^t_c) لكل مائة ألف من السكان في منتصف السنة (P). ويُحسب كالتالي:

14- متوسط العمر عند الزواج الأول

وهو متوسط العمر لأي فرد عند الزواج الأول في سنة معينة باستخدام معدلات الزواج الأول في السن (أي عدد الزيجات في السن (x) نسبة إلى متوسط عدد السكان في هذه الطريقة في الحساب لا يؤخذ بعين الاعتبار عدد النساء أو الرجال في كل سن.

15- معدل الزواج الخام

وهو نسبة عدد الزيجات في منطقة معينة خلال سنة معينة (أو المتوسط السنوي خلال فترة معينة)(M^t_o) إلى متوسط عدد السكان (P) في المنطقة نفسها والفترة نفسها لكل ألف من السكان. ويُحسب كالتالي:

16. Crude divorce rate (Cdiv)

The ratio of the number of divorces in a given area during a calendar year (or annual average across a given period) (Div $^t_0$) to the average population (P) in the same period and the same area per 1,000 inhabitants:

$$Cdiv = \frac{Div^t_0}{P} \times 1000$$

16- معدل الطلاق الخام

وهو نسبة عدد حالات الطلاق في منطقة معينة خلال سنة معينة (أو المتوسط السنوي خلال فترة معينة) (Div $^t_0$) إلى متوسط عدد السكان (P) في المنطقة نفسها والفترة نفسها لكل ألف من السكان. ويحسب كالتالي:

GLOSSARY OF STATISTICAL TERMS

Age-specific fertility rate

Number of births to women in a particular age group, divided by the number of women in that age group. The age groups used are 15-19, 20-24, 25-29, 30-34, 35-39, 40-44 and 45-49. The data refer to five-year periods running from 1 July of the initial year to 30 June of the final year.

Base population

The number of people in a given area (for example, a nation, province or city) to which a specific vital rate applies; that is, the denominator of the crude birth rate or death rate, the population being determined from census data.

Births

Average annual number of births over a given period. The data refer to five-year periods running from 1 July of the initial year to 30 June of the final year and data are presented in thousands.

Births by age group of mother

Number of births over a given period classified by age group of mother (15-19, 20-24, 25-29, 30-34, 35-39, 40-44 and 45-49). The data refer to five-year periods running from 1 July of the initial year to 30 June of the final year. Data are presented in thousands.

Census

A survey conducted on the full set of observation objects belonging to a given population or universe.

مسرد المصطلحات الإحصائية

معدل الخصوبة العمرية

عدد المواليد لنساء من فئة عمرية معينة مقسوماً على عدد النساء من تلك الفئة. والفئات العمرية المستخدمة هي: 15-19 سنة، و24-20 سنة، و29-25 سنة، و34-30 سنة، و39-35 سنة، و44-40 سنة، و49-45 سنة. وتشير البيانات إلى فترات من خمس سنوات تبدأ في 1 تموز/يوليو من سنة البداية وتنتهي في 30 حزيران/يونيو من سنة النهاية.

القاعدة السكانية

عدد السكان في منطقة معينة (مثل بلد أو مقاطعة أو مدينة) في معدل حيوي معين، أي أنه القاسم من معدل الوفيات، حيث يحدد عدد السكان من بيانات التعداد.

الولادات

المتوسط السنوي لعدد الولادات خلال فترة معينة. وتشير البيانات التي ترد بالآلاف، إلى فترات من خمس سنوات تبدأ في 1 تموز/يوليو من سنة البداية وتنتهي في 30 حزيران/يونيو من سنة النهاية.

الولادات بحسب الفئة العمرية للأم

عدد الولادات خلال فترة معينة مصنفة بحسب الفئة العمرية للأم (15-19) سنة، و24-20 سنة، و29-25 سنة، و39-35 سنة، و44-40 سنة، و49-45 سنة. وتشير البيانات التي ترد بالآلاف، إلى فترات من خمس سنوات تبدأ في 1 تموز/يوليو من سنة البداية وتنتهي في 30 حزيران/يونيو من سنة النهاية.

التعداد

مسح يجرى حول مجموعة كاملة من المواصفات المشمولة بالمراقبة والتي تعبر سكان معينين أو عالماً معيناً.

Census population	تعداد السكان
Latest census population, covering all residents, regardless of legal status or citizenship, except for refugees not permanently settled in the country of asylum. Data are presented by nationals and non nationals, by sex, and by rural and urban areas per country. In addition, census population data for each of the above disaggregations are presented by five-year age group for each country.	آخر تعداد للسكان يشمل كل المقيمين، بصرف النظر عن وضعهم القانوني أو جنسيتهم، باستثناء اللاجئين غير المقيمين بشكل دائم في بلد اللجوء. وترد البيانات بحسب المواطنين وغير المواطنين، وبحسب النوع الاجتماعي، والمناطق الريفية والحضرية لكل بلد. وبالإضافة إلى ذلك ترد البيانات حول كل من هذه الجوانب وفق فئات عمرية من خمس سنوات لكل بلد.
Crude birth rate	معدل المواليد الخام
Number of births over a given year per 1,000 population.	عدد المواليد في سنة معينة لكل ألف من السكان.
Crude death rate	معدل الوفيات الخام
Number of deaths over a given year per 1,000 population.	عدد الوفيات في سنة معينة لكل ألف من السكان.
Crude marriage rate	معدل الزواج الخام
The number of marriages occurring in the population of a given geographical area during a given year per 1,000 mid-year total population of the given area during the same year.	عدد الزيجات التي تحدث بين سكان منطقة جغرافية معينة خلال سنة معينة لكل ألف من السكان في منتصف السنة لتلك المنطقة وخلال تلك السنة.
Deaths by sex	الوفيات بحسب الجنس
Number of deaths over a given period, classified by sex (male, female and both sexes combined). The data refer to five-year periods running from 1 July of the initial year to 30 June of the final year and data are presented in thousands.	عدد الوفيات خلال فترة معينة مصنفة بحسب النوع الاجتماعي (أي الذكور والإناث والفئتان معاً). وتشير البيانات التي ترد بالألاف، إلى فترات من خمس سنوات تبدأ في 1 تموز/يوليو من سنة البداية وتنتهي في 30 حزيران/يونيو من سنة النهاية.
Deaths under age 1	الوفيات دون السنة من العمر
Number of deaths under age 1 over a given period. The data refer to five-year periods running from 1 July of the initial year to 30 June of the final year and data are presented in thousands.	عدد الوفيات التي تحدث قبل بلوغ السنة الأولى من العمر خلال فترة معينة. وتشير البيانات التي ترد بالألاف، إلى فترات من خمس سنوات تبدأ في 1 تموز/يوليو من سنة البداية وتنتهي في 30 حزيران/يونيو من سنة النهاية.

Deaths under age 5	Number of deaths under age 5 over a given period. The data refer to five-year periods running from 1 July of the initial year to 30 June of the final year. Data are presented in thousands.	الوفيات دون سن الخامسة	عدد الوفيات التي تحدث قبل بلوغ السنة الخامسة من العمر خلال فترة معينة. وتشير البيانات التي ترد بالآلاف، إلى فترات من خمس سنوات تبدأ في 1 تموز/يوليو من سنة البداية وتنتهي في 30 حزيران/يونيو من سنة النهاية.
Dependency ratios	The total dependency ratio is the ratio of the sum of the population aged 0-14 plus that aged 65 and over to the population aged 15-64. The child dependency ratio is the ratio of the population aged 0-14 to the population aged 15-64. The old-age dependency ratio is the ratio of the population aged 65 years and over to the population aged 15-64. All ratios are presented as number of dependants per 100 persons of working age (15-64).	نسب الإعالة	نسبة الإعالة الكلية هي نسبة مجموع عدد السكان بعمر 14 سنة وعدد السكان بعمر 65 سنة وما فوق إلى عدد السكان بعمر 15 إلى 64 سنة. ونسبة إعالة الأطفال هي نسبة عدد السكان بعمر صفر إلى 14 سنة إلى عدد السكان بعمر 15 إلى 64 سنة. ونسبة إعالة المسنين هي نسبة عدد السكان بعمر 65 سنة وما فوق إلى عدد السكان بعمر 15 إلى 64 سنة. وترد كل النسب كعدد المعالين لكل مائة شخص بعمر العمل أي من 15 إلى 64 سنة.
Divorce	The final dissolution of a marriage, that is, the separation of husband and wife which confers on the parties the right to remarriage under civil, religious and/or other provisions, according to the laws of each country.	الطلاق	الفسخ النهائي للزواج، أي انفصال الزوج والزوجة على نحو يعطي الطرفين حق الزواج من جديد بموجب أحكام مدنية و/أو دينية و/أو أحكام أخرى، وفقا لقوانين كل بلد.
Estimation	The process of inferring the numerical value of unknown population values from incomplete data, such as a sample.	التقدير	عملية استنتاج قيمة القيم سكانية مجهولة من خلال بيانات غير مكتملة، مثل النموذج.
First marriage rates by age	The number of first marriages of women (or men) of age x in relation to the average female (or male) population of age x. Depending on the country, the age is either the age reached during the year or the age at last birthday.	معدلات الزواج الأول بحسب العمر	عدد الزيجات الأولى للنساء (أو الرجال) في سن (x) نسبة إلى متوسط عدد الإناث (أو الذكور) من السكان في سن (x). وتكون السن، بحسب البلد المعني، إما السن التي تم بلوغها في آخر عيد ميلاد، أو السن المعنية خلال السنة.

المصطلح	التعريف	Term	Definition
وفيات الرضع	أرجحية وفاة طفل مولود في سنة معينة قبل بلوغه السنة الأولى من عمره، إذا انطبقت عليه المعدلات السائدة للوفيات بحسب الأعمار. وتقاس بعدد الوفيات لكل ألف من الأحياء.	**Infant mortality**	The probability (expressed as deaths per 1,000 live births) of a child born in a specified year dying before reaching the age of 1 if subject to current age-specific mortality rates.
العمر المتوقع بحسب الجنس	متوسط عدد السنوات التي من المتوقع أن يعيشها فوج من المتوفين الأفراد إذا انطبقت عليهم، طوال حياتهم، معدلات الوفيات في فترة معينة، ويقاس بالسنوات.	**Life expectancy by sex**	The average number of years of life expected by a hypothetical cohort of individuals if subject throughout their lives to the mortality rates of a given period, expressed in years.
الزواج	العمل أو الاحتفال أو الإجراء الذي ينشأ بموجبه الرباط الشرعي بين الزوج والزوجة. وينشأ هذا الرباط بطرق مدنية أو دينية أو غيرها، نما للقوانين المعمول بها في كل بلد.	**Marriage**	The act, ceremony or process by which the legal relationship of husband and wife is constituted. The legality of the union may be established by civil, religious or other means, as recognized by the laws of each country.
متوسط العمر عند الزواج الأول	المتوسط المرجّح للعمر عند الزواج الأول ويحسب باستخدام معدلات الزواج العمرية للزيجات الأولى فقط كعوامل مرجحة.	**Mean age at first marriage**	The weighted average of the age at first marriage, using as weights the age-specific marriage rates for first marriages only.
الوفاة قبل سن الخامسة من العمر	أرجحية حدوث الوفاة في وقت بين الولادة والسنة الخامسة من العمر، وتحسب بعدد الوفيات لكل ألف من المواليد.	**Mortality under age 5**	Probability of death between birth and fifth birthday, expressed as deaths per 1,000 births.
معدل الإحلال الصافي	متوسط عدد المواليد الإناث لفوج افتراضي من النساء في نهاية فترتهن الإنجابية إذا انطبقت عليهن طوال حياتهن معدلات الخصوبة ومعدلات الوفاة لفترة معينة، ويحسب كعدد المواليد الإناث لكل امرأة.	**Net reproduction rate**	The average number of daughters a hypothetical cohort of women would have at the end of their reproductive period if they were subject throughout their lives to the fertility rates and mortality rates of a given period, expressed as number of daughters per woman.
النسبة المئوية الحضرية	سكان المناطق الحضرية كنسبة مئوية من مجموع السكان.	**Percentage urban**	Urban population as a percentage of the total population.
النسبة المئوية الريفية	سكان المناطق الريفية كنسبة مئوية من مجموع السكان.	**Percentage rural**	Rural population as a percentage of the total population.

مكان الحدوث — جزء من التقسيم المدني لبلد معين، أي المقاطعة أو الإقليم أو البلدية أو الإدارة أو الولاية الحية حيث تحدث الوفاة أو وفاة الجنين أو الزواج أو الطلاق.	**Place of occurrence** — The civil subdivision of a country (district, county, municipality, province, department or state) in which a live birth or death, foetal death, marriage or divorce takes place.
نسبة الجنس من السكان — عدد الذكور لكل مئة أنثى من السكان.	**Population sex ratio** — Number of males per 100 females in the population.
السكان — العدد الفعلي لسكان بلد أو نطاق أو منطقة ما في 1 تموز/يوليو من السنة المعنية. وترد البيانات بالآلاف.	**Population** — De facto population of a country, area or region as at 1 July of the year indicated. Figures are presented in thousands.
السكان حسب الفئة العمرية — العدد الفعلي للسكان في 1 تموز/يوليو من السنة المعنية للفئة العمرية المعينة (وترد البيانات بالآلاف) والنسبة المئوية للسكان التي يمثلها هذا العدد من مجموع السكان. والفئات العمرية للسكان هي: صفر-4، صفر-14، 5-14، 6-11، 12-14، 15-17، 18-23، 15-24، 15-59، 15-64، 60 وما فوق، 65 وما فوق و80 وما فوق.	**Population by age group** — De facto population as at 1 July of the year indicated for the age group indicated (presented in thousands), and the percentage of the total population that it represents. The population age groups are: 0-4, 0-14, 5-14, 6-11, 12-14, 15-17, 18-23, 15-24, 15-59, 15-64, 60 or over, 65 or over and 80 or over.
السكان المعرّضون — مجموع السكان المعرّضون لحدوث واقعة حيوية، وعلى سبيل المثال، السكان المعرّضون قانونيا إذا كان الأمر يتعلق بحالات الطلاق.	**Population at risk** — The population that is exposed to the occurrence of a vital event, for example, the total population in the case of deaths or the legally-married population in the case of divorces.
السكان حسب فئات عمرية من خمس سنوات والجنس — العدد الفعلي للسكان في 1 تموز/يوليو من السنة المعنية، محسّنون بحسب النوع الاختناعي (أي الذكور والإناث)، وبحسب فئات عمرية من خمس سنوات (صفر-4 سنوات، و5 إلى 9 سنوات، و10 إلى 14 سنة، [...] 95 إلى 99 سنة و100 سنة وما فوق). وترد البيانات بالآلاف.	**Population by five-year age group and sex** — De facto population as at 1 July of the year indicated, classified by sex (male, female and both sexes combined) and by five-year age groups (0-4, 5-9, 10-14 [...] 95-99, 100+). Data are presented in thousands.

Term	Definition	المصطلح	التعريف
Population census	The process of collecting, compiling, evaluating, analyzing and publishing or otherwise disseminating demographic, economic and social data pertaining, at a specified time, to all persons in a country or in a well-delimited part of a country.	تعداد السكان	عملية جمع وتجهيز وتقييم وتحليل ونشر أو توزيع البيانات المتعلقة بالخصائص الديمغرافية والاقتصادية والاجتماعية لجميع الأفراد داخل بلد معين أو جزء محدد جيداً من البلد وفي زمن معين.
Population estimates	Country estimates, disaggregated by sex, presented in a time series from 2000 until 2007.	التقديرات السكانية	التقديرات السكانية للبلدان معنفة بحسب النوع الاجتماعي، وبقدمة لسلاسل زمنية من عام 2000 إلى عام 2007.
Population projections	Estimates of total size or composition of populations in the future.	التوقعات السكانية	التقديرات بشأن ما سيكون عليه الحجم الإجمالي للسكان أو تركيبهم في المستقبل.
Proportion	A special type of ratio in which the denominator is a quantity that represents the whole of a given group under investigation and the numerator is a subset of it.	النسبة	نوع خاص من النسبة حيث يكون القاسم كمية تمثل مجمل الفئة المعنية المشمولة بالبحث، وحيث يكون البسط هو جزء منها.
Rate	The occurrence of events over a specific interval. Also refers to the measure of the frequency of a phenomenon of interest.	المعدل	حدوث وقائع ما خلال فترة فاصلة محددة. وهو أيضاً قياس تردد ظاهرة اهتمام معينة.
Rate of natural increase	Crude birth rate minus crude death rate. Represents the portion of population growth (or decline) determined exclusively by births and deaths.	معدل الزيادة الطبيعية	معدل المواليد الخام ناقصاً معدل الوفيات الخام، وهو يمثل جزءاً من النمو السكاني تحدده الولادات والوفيات فقط.
Ratio	The relationship between two quantities measured in the same unit, expressed as one value divided by another. The result has no unit.	النسبة	العلاقة بين كميتين تقاسان بالوحدة القياسية ذاتها، محسوبة نسبة إحدى القيمتين على الأخرى. وليس للنسبة وحدة قياس.

English	Definition	Arabic term	Arabic definition
Registration of vital events	Continuous, ...ent and compulsory recording of ...ccurrence of vital events, together with c... identifying or descriptive characteristics re... to such events, regulated by the civil cod... or regulations of each country. Such v...ts may include live births, deaths, foe..., marriages, divorces, judicial separatio..., marriage annulments, adoptions, recognitions (legal acknowledgement of natural children) and legitimations.	تسجيل الوقائع الحيوية	التسجيل المستمر والإلزامي والدائم لحدوث الوقائع الحيوية، بالإضافة إلى تحديد الخصائص المميزة أو الوصفية لتلك الوقائع، وتنظيمها بمقتضى القوانين أو الأنظمة المدنية في كل بلد. وقد تشمل هذه الوقائع المواليد الأحياء، والوفيات، والأجنة، والزواج، وحالات الطلاق (الانفصال القضائي)، وفسخ الزواج، والتبني، والاعتراف (الإقرار القانوني بالأطفال الطبيعيين) وإثبات النسب.
Rural population	De facto population living in areas classified as rural (that is, the difference between the total population of a country and its urban population). Data refer to 1 July of the year indicated and are presented in thousands.	سكان الريف	عدد السكان الفعليين المقيمين في المناطق المصنفة كريف (أي الفرق بين مجموع سكان البلد وسكانها الحضر). وتشير البيانات إلى 1 تموز/يوليه من السنة المشار إليها، وهي معروضة بالآلاف.
Sex ratio at birth	Number of male births per single female birth.	نسبة الجنس عند الولادة	عدد المواليد الذكور لكل مولودة.
Total fertility rate	The average number of children a hypothetical cohort of women would have at the end of their reproductive period if they were subject throughout their lives to the fertility rates of a given period and not subject to mortality; expressed as number of children per woman.	معدل الخصوبة الكلي	متوسط عدد الأطفال الذين ستنجبهم مجموعة افتراضية من النساء في نهاية فترتهن الإنجابية إذا أخضعن طوال حياتهن لمعدلات الخصوبة في فترة معينة ولم يخضعن للوفيات؛ ويعبر عن هذا المعدل بعدد الأطفال لكل امرأة.
Total first marriage rate	The mean number of first marriages in a given year, calculated by adding the first marriage rates by age of women (or men) for the year in question. For the purposes of calculation, the number of women (or men) at each age is assumed to be the same. It does not separate out the different generations and is not the first marriage rate of any specific generation; rather, it is the first marriage rate of a hypothetical generation subjected at each age to the current marriage conditions.	معدل الزواج الأول الكلي	متوسط عدد الزيجات الأولى في سنة معينة، محسوباً بإضافة معدلات الزواج الأول حسب عمر النساء (أو الرجال) للسنة المعنية. ولأغراض الحساب، يفترض أن عدد النساء (أو الرجال) في كل عمر هو نفسه، فهو لا يفصل بين مختلف الأجيال، وليس معدل الزواج الأول لأي جيل محدد؛ بل هو معدل الزواج الأول لجيل افتراضي يخضع في كل عمر لشروط الزواج الحالية.

Urban population

Given national differences in the characteristics that distinguish urban from rural areas, the distinction between urban and rural population is not amenable to a single definition applicable to all countries. National definitions are commonly based on size of locality; any population that is not urban is considered rural.

سكان الحضر

نظراً للاختلافات الوطنية في الخصائص التي تميز الحضر عن المناطق الريفية، فإن التمييز بين سكان الحضر والسكان الريفيين لا يخضع لتعريف واحد يمكن تطبيقه على جميع البلدان. والتعاريف الوطنية عادة ما تستند إلى حجم المحلية؛ وأي سكان لا يعد من سكان الحضر يعتبر من سكان الريف.

Vital event

A live birth, death, foetal death, marriage, divorce, adoption, legitimation, recognition of parenthood, annulment of marriage or legal separation.

واقعة حيوية

ولادة حية، أو وفاة، أو وفاة الجنين، أو الزواج، أو الطلاق، أو التبني، أو الاعتراف بالأبوة، أو إبطال الزواج أو الانفصال القانوني.

Women aged 15-49

Number of women aged 15-49 as at 1 July of the year indicated (presented in thousands) and that number as a percentage of the total female population as at 1 July of that year.

النساء اللاتي تتراوح أعمارهن بين 15 و 49

عدد النساء اللاتي تتراوح أعمارهن بين 15 و 49 سنة في 1 تموز/يوليه من السنة المبينة (بالآلاف)، وذلك العدد كنسبة مئوية من مجموع السكان الإناث في 1 تموز/يوليه من تلك السنة.